THE GIRL WHO MADE STARS

AND OTHER BUSHMEN STORIES

The Girl Who Made Stars

and Other Bushmen Stories

Collected by Wilhelm Bleek and Lucy C. Lloyd

Edited by Gregory McNamee

DAIMON
VERLAG

The stories in *The Girl Who Made Stars* are adapted from texts gathered by W. H. I. Bleek and published in W. H. I. Bleek and L. C. Lloyd, *Specimens of Bushmen Folklore* (London: George Allen & Co, Ltd., 1911; new edition in Daimon Verlag, Einsiedeln, 2001).

The full text of the original English translation as well as a complete transcription of the Bushman language version of the stories in this volume are available in a 576-page facsimile edition: *Specimens of Bushmen Folklore* collected by W. H. I. Bleek and L. C. Lloyd, Daimon, Einsiedeln, 2001, ISBN 3-85630-603-X.

Modern English versions in this edition copyright © 2001 by Gregory McNamee.

ISBN 3-85630-599-8

Copyright © 2001 Daimon Verlag, Einsiedeln

Cover illustration: Bushman drawings of a hartebeest and two steinboks (see p. 228 of *Specimens of Bushmen Folklore*) and an illustration to a story where a food tree grows out of the wife's head (see p. 325, *ibid.*)

There is a dream dreaming us.

– Bushmen saying

Contents

Songs

Hunters

Dreams and Beliefs

ǀhanǂkass'o, one of the Bushmen storytellers

Introduction

In 1857, a thirty-year-old German linguist named Wilhelm Bleek traveled to the Cape Colony, in what is now the Republic of South Africa, to visit his émigré brother and his family. Trained as a philologist, Bleek had prepared himself for the trip by studying the grammars of several indigenous languages; when he arrived, he carefully reviewed earlier linguists' work, finding native speakers and asking them to correct problems of pronunciation and usage that he had found in the scholarly literature.

In this way, Bleek painstakingly achieved a working knowledge of several languages of southern Africa. All posed difficulties for the outsider, Bleek noted, but none was quite so challenging as the Khoisan tongue of the people called Boesjemans, or Bushmen, a tongue that gave phonemic value to an array of "clicks," glottal stops, and other sounds that were baffling to European ears. Bleek pressed on, developing an orthography for the Bushmen dialects he encountered and writing learned articles about them for scholarly journals in Germany and England.

In his study of these languages and their variants, following the model of his near-contemporaries Jacob and Wilhelm Grimm and working with his brilliant sister-in-law, Lucy Lloyd, Bleek collected a large body of folktales. Most of them came from Bushmen narrators who had been born in the interior but brought to the Cape Colony, almost always against their will. Many of his consultants were, in fact, prisoners who had been jailed for the offense of having done nothing more than following their way of life – hunting on ancestral lands suddenly declared off-limits to them, refusing to abandon practices developed over countless millennia, evading the directives of traveling missionaries and government officials. Bleek's friend Xhabbo, "The Dream," was one such man; cut off from his wife and children, far from the hills and saltpans of the interior, Xhabbo recited stories he had learned as a child, reminisced about his encounters with unpredictably dangerous animals and predictably dangerous people, and quietly lamented the fact that in his remote English prison the stories that had arrived to him in the desert, as if carried by the wind, could no longer find him.

The stories Xhabbo and other Bushmen gave to Bleek were small masterpieces, marvels of storytelling economy, charged with meaning, metaphorical and beautiful. In these stories, the captive Bushmen who once followed game through the vast, arid interior spoke of the sometimes treacherous behavior of the Mantis, the insect god who assisted at the creation and gave names to things. They explained the origin of the stars, which give light to the people so that they can find their way home, and the origin of death, the outcome of a hare's foolishness. They warned of the many dangers that the world poses, whether in the form of marauding baboons or lethal lightning. They revealed the meaning of dreams and the ways of their people. And, quietly and elegantly, they made it clear that their knowledge of such things gave them a pressing claim to exist and to be left in peace.

Sitting in his brother's windswept garden, notebook in hand, Wilhelm Bleek listened to these stories with a linguist's practiced concentration, striving to record the smallest nuances of pronunciation and grammar, to transcribe the faintest nasalization and the sharpest lateral fricative. The meaning of the utterances he gathered was, in the early

Xhabbo, Dr. Bleek's Bushman Teacher

Díä\kwain, another Bushman Storyteller

|kweiten ta ||kên, sister of Díä|kwain
She narrated some of these stories

months of his work, of secondary interest to him, but in time, in the company of Xhabbo and his friends, Bleek came to listen to the texts spellbound. Eliciting clarifications, retellings, and alternate versions, he gathered several books' worth of Bushmen stories, almost all of them published after listener and speaker alike had died – for, felled by disease and the terrible loneliness of imprisonment, Xhabbo died in 1873, and Bleek joined him in death only two years later.

The body of work Bleek and Lucy Lloyd collected is now generally regarded as the single most reliable body of ethnographic evidence for traditional Bushman culture, and it remains at the heart of the scattered anthropological literature devoted to the first peoples of the Kalahari. Laurens van der Post, the great South African writer and ethnographer whose work both drew on and augmented that of Bleek and Lloyd, observed in *The Heart of the Hunter* that these stories contain a universe of detail that would otherwise be unknown to us, and that, although lions and elephants and other large creatures figure prominently in them, they reveal a wealth of information about the actors that European science too often overlooks: the procession of the stars and planets, the ways of ants, the movement of elands and gemsboks from one watering hole to another, the rustling of dry reeds in the hot wind, and the solitude of ghosts.

One of the books Bleek and Lloyd made of their work was published in London, in 1911, as *Specimens of Bushmen Folklore*. That book underlies this one: each of the stories in *The Girl Who Made Stars* corresponds to one in the original collection. A small difference is that in the present book the stories are grouped thematically. A larger difference, which will be immediately noticeable to readers of Bleek and Lloyd's original, is that these stories are here rendered in a contemporary, literary English that departs markedly from the nineteenth-century versions, in which Bleek and Lloyd attempted

14

to convey the sometimes orotund, sometimes elliptical, and often repetitive rhetorical features of traditional Bushman expression, arriving at a kind of hybrid speech that was not quite English and not quite Bushman, but a curious blend of both.

Their method remains of considerable interest to students of oral literature, but it is of less immediate concern to readers whose wish is simply to hear a good story. Both publisher and editor hope in this book to honor Bleek and Lloyd's extraordinary work while creating a text that would appeal to readers without prior knowledge of Bushmen ways of life – and certainly without formal training in linguistics. We hope that these retellings of their texts have not in any way betrayed Bleek and Lloyd's intentions or done violence to the stories they gathered, stories that are always more complex than they appear to be on first glance.

The time when Wilhelm Bleek and Lucy Lloyd did their work has long passed. With it, the world of the Bushmen on whom those sympathetic Europeans relied has now very nearly disappeared. Bleek observed of the Bushmen that in his day "every man's hand was against them," and that their every hour was laden with peril. Matters did not much improve for succeeding generations, as thousands of Bushmen were murdered or driven away from their lands. It is thought that perhaps only forty individuals are now alive who preserve intact traditional ways of life and knowledge; still not free to move at will across the countryside, these forty reside within South Africa's Kagga Kamma Game Reserve, where they live astride two worlds: that of the ancient past, and the ever more closely approaching global monoculture that has erased so many cultures in the space of a few decades.

When those forty are gone, a way of life that has endured for fifty centuries, and perhaps even longer, will disappear with them. It will be but one of the myriad such quiet disappearances that mark our time, the disappearances of languages, animal and plant species, habitats. We can only hope, as Xhabbo gently suggested, that the Bushmen will remain in the world forever, their bodies having taken the guise of trailing, beautiful, ever-transforming clouds.

Let us close with a note on the perils of terminology. The term *Bushman* has a long history, first used by Dutch arrivals in southern Africa to refer, more or less collectively, to the indigenous peoples who lived inland from the coast – that is, in "the bush." In recent years a view has emerged that the introduced word *Bushman* carries pejorative connotations and should therefore be avoided. Some anthropologists and activists have suggested that *San* take its place. This replacement, however, is equally problematic, for *San*, which comes from the Nama language of Namibia, is a blanket term that means, the anthropologist Elizabeth Marshall Thomas observes, "someone who is poor, lives in the bush, has no livestock, and eats food from the ground." The San-speaking peoples in question have no collective term for themselves in their own languages; instead, they use ethnic terms such as !Xo, Juwasi, and Nahara for individual groups and Bushmen for the collectivity. Following Wilhelm Bleek and Lucy Lloyd, this usage is observed in this book.

GREGORY MCNAMEE
Tucson, Arizona
Autumn, 2000

Animal Stories

The Mantis Assumes the Form of a Hartebeest

The Mantis, the creator god, cheated the children by pretending to be a dead hartebeest. He pretended to be dead. He lay on a path where the children were walking in search of wild cucumbers. He had a plan. He wanted the children to cut him up with a stone knife.

The children saw him. He looked dead, stretched out in the dust, his horns turned backward. The children said, "There is a dead hartebeest." The children rejoiced, saying, "Our hartebeest! We will eat great meat."

They broke off stone knives by striking one stone against another, and they skinned the Mantis. The skin of the Mantis snatched itself out of the children's hands. The children said to each other, "Hold the hartebeest skin still for me!" One child said, "The hartebeest skin pulled away from me."

Her elder sister said: "It seems that the hartebeest was not shot, for it has no wound. The hartebeest appears to have died for no reason. Although the hartebeest is fat, it has no wound."

The elder sister cut off a shoulder of the hartebeest and set it down on a bush. The hartebeest's shoulder arose by itself and sat down on the other side of the bush. The elder sister cut off one of the hartebeest's thighs and put it down on a bush. She cut off a shoulder and put it on another bush. The shoulder arose by itself and sat on a soft part of the bush, as if it had been made uncomfortable by thorns.

Another sister cut off the other thigh. The sisters spoke: "This hartebeest's flesh moves. It shrinks away from us."

One sister said to the other, "Cut and break off the harte-beest's neck, so that our younger sister can carry the harte-beest's head. Our elder sister can carry the hartebeest's back, for she is a big girl. We must bring it home. Its flesh moves; its flesh snatches itself out of our hands. It moves by itself."

The sisters took up the Mantis's flesh. They said to the youngest child, "Carry the hartebeest's head. When you get home, father will roast it for you." The youngest child lifted the hartebeest's head, calling to her sisters, "Help me up. This hartebeest's head is not light!" Her sisters helped her up.

They went away, returning home. The hartebeest's head slipped downward off the child's back. It wanted to stand on the ground. The youngest child hoisted it up on her shoulders with a leather thong. The hartebeest's head, by turning a little, removed the thong from its eye. The hartebeest's head whis-pered, whispered to the child, "O child! The thong is in my eye. Take it away. The thong is cutting into my eye."

The youngest child looked behind her. The Mantis winked. The child whimpered. Her elder sister looked back at her. Her elder sister called to her, "Come quickly! Let's get home."

The child exclaimed, "This hartebeest's head is able to speak." Her elder sister scolded her, saying, "Don't lie to us!" The child said to her elder sister, "The hartebeest winked at me and asked me to take the thong from his eye." The child looked back at the hartebeest's head, the hartebeest opened and shut its eyes. The child said to her elder sister, "The hartebeest's head must be alive, for it is opening and shutting its eyes."

The child, walking on, loosened the thong and let the hartebeest's head fall to the ground. The Mantis scolded the child, complaining, "Oh! Oh! My head! Oh! Bad little person! Hurting me in my head."

Her sisters dropped the Mantis's limbs. The flesh of the Mantis sprang together, it quickly joined itself to the lower part of the Mantis's back. The head of the Mantis quickly joined itself to the Mantis's spine. The upper part of the Mantis's spine joined itself to the Mantis's back. The thigh of the Mantis sprang forward and joined itself to the Mantis's back. His other thigh ran forward and joined itself to the other side of the Mantis's back. The chest of the Mantis ran forward; it jointed itself to the front side of the upper part of the Mantis's spine. The shoulder blade of the Mantis ran forward; it joined itself to the ribs of the Mantis. The other shoulder blade of the Mantis ran forward.

The children ran away. The Mantis arose from the ground and ran, chasing the children. He was whole again, and he raced along. The children raced ahead of him.

He saw that the children had reached home. The Mantis turned and descended to the river. He went along the riverbed, making a noise as he stepped in the soft sand. He ran alongside the river. He returned to his own home.

The children said, "We saw a hartebeest that was dead. That hartebeest, it was dead. That hartebeest, we cut it up with stone knives; its flesh quivered. The hartebeest's flesh snatched itself out of our hands. It moved itself onto some comfortable bushes. Its head whispered to our little sister there while she was carrying it." The youngest child said to her father: "O papa! Don't you believe that the hartebeest's head talked to me? It did! It lay on my shoulder and told me to remove the thong from its eye."

Her father said to them: "Have you seen and cut up the old man, the Mantis, while he lay pretending to be dead in front of you?"

The children said, "We thought it was dead. The hartebeest talked to us and chased us when we put its body down. The hartebeest's flesh jumped together. It made itself whole again. And when he saw that we reached the house, he whisked around. He ran, kicked up his heels, showing the white soles

21

of his shoes, and he ran before the wind, he ran with all his might into the riverbed, he ran over that hill there."

Their parents said to the children: "You went and cut up the old man Tinderbox-Owner, the Mantis, the creator. He was one who came out from the place behind the hill."

The children said, "He ran home. He will deceive us again. We will cut him up with stone knives. He feigned death so that he could chase us. Now we are tired, and our hearts burn with weariness. We will no longer go hunting for food. Instead, we will stay home."

Gaunu-tsaxau, the Baboons, and the Mantis

Gaunu-tsaxau, the son of the Mantis, once went to fetch sticks for his father, so that his father could take aim at the people who sit upon their heels.

Gaunu-tsaxau went up to the baboons as they were going along feeding themselves. He approached an old baboon who was feeding. The old baboon questioned Gaunu-tsaxau. And Gaunu-tsaxau told him that he had to fetch sticks for his father, so that his father could take aim at the people who sit upon their heels. The old baboon exclaimed, "Hie! Come to listen to this child." Another baboon, speaking in the language of those people, said:

> *First going*
> *I listen*
> *To the child yonder.*

> *First going*
> *I listen,*
> *To the child yonder.*

The old baboon took Gaunu-tsaxau to another baboon, who also sang,

> *First going*
> *I listen,*
> *To the child yonder.*

First going
I listen,
To the child yonder.

The old baboon and Gaunu-tsaxau went to still another baboon, who asked, "What does this child say?" And the old baboon answered, "This child wants, he says, to fetch sticks for his father, so that his father may take aim at the people who sit upon their heels." The other baboon exclaimed, "He means us!"

The old baboon exclaimed, "What? It is us that he means? Strike that child with your fists!"

The baboons beat Gaunu-tsaxau with their fists. They broke his head. And another struck Gaunu-tsaxau with his fist, knocking out Gaunu-tsaxau's eye. The eye rolled away into the bushes. Then the baboon who hit Gaunu-tsaxau exclaimed, "My ball! My ball!" The baboons began to play a game of ball, while Gaunu-tsaxau died. Gaunu-tsaxau lay still. The baboons sang:

I want it.
Whose ball is it?

I want it.
Whose ball is it?
I want it.

The other people said:

My companion's ball it is,
And I want it,
My companion's ball it is,
And I want it.

They sang while they were playing ball there with Gaunu-tsaxau's eye.

The Mantis was waiting for the child. The Mantis lay down at noon. He dreamed about the child. He dreamed that the baboons had killed the child, that they had made a ball of the child's eye, and that he went to the baboons while the baboons played ball with the child's eye.

The Mantis arose. He took up his quiver, intoning: "Rattling along, rattling along, rattling along, rattling along."

When he came into sight of the baboons' camp, he saw a cloud of dust that the baboons made as they played ball with Gaunu-tsaxau's eye. Then the Mantis cried, because the baboons appeared to have killed the child. But he quickly shut his mouth and dried the tears from his eyes, because he did not want the baboons to see that he had been crying.

He set down his quiver and took off his leather cloak. Then he ran up to the baboons. Startled, the baboons stared at him. He began to play with the ball. He called out to the baboons, asking why it was that the baboons were staring at him, why it was that the baboons were not playing with the ball. The Mantis hollered that if they were finished playing with it they should throw the ball to him.

Then the baboons looked at one another, because they suspected why he said such things. Mantis caught hold of the ball. Then the child's eye, also startled, became aware of his father's scent. The baboons chased around, trying to get the ball. Then one baboon caught it and passed it to another baboon. Mantis sprang out and caught hold of the child's eye again. Then the Mantis whirled the child's eye around, anointing it with the sweat of his armpits. He threw the child's eye toward the baboons. The child's eye ascended, the child's eye went about in the sky; the baboons beheld it there, rolling around in the sky above. The child's eye went and stood beside the Mantis's quiver.

The baboons chased after it, trying to catch the eye. So did the Mantis. The baboons said, "Give my companion the ball," "Give me the ball." The Mantis said, "Behold! I do not have the ball." The baboons said, "Give my companion the ball." The old baboon said, "Give me the ball." Then the baboons ordered the Mantis to shake his quiver, for the ball seemed to be inside it. And the Mantis exclaimed, "Behold! Behold! The ball is not inside the bag. Behold!" He held the child's eye in his hand while he shook the quiver inside out. He said, "Behold! Behold! The ball cannot be inside the bag."

Then the old baboon exclaimed, "Hit that old man with your fists!" The other baboons cried, "Give my companion the ball!" And one of them struck the Mantis's head. Then the Mantis exclaimed, "I have not got the ball," while he struck the baboon's head in return.

The Mantis got the worst of it. He exclaimed: "Ow! Hartebeest's children, my leather quiver! We must go! We must go!" The baboons watched him ascend as he flew up.

The Mantis flew to the water. He popped into the water to wash his wounds. Then he walked out of the water. He sat down; he felt inside his bag; he took out the child's eye; he walked on as he held it; he walked up to the grass at the top of the water's bank, and he sat down again. He exclaimed, "Ow! Oh! Ho!" as he put the child's eye into the water. "You must grow again, you must become like what you were before." Then he walked on. He took up his quiver and threw it over his shoulder, and he went home.

Then young Ichneumon, Mantis's snake-eating grandson, exclaimed, "Who can have done this to my grandfather, the Mantis, who is covered with wounds?" The Mantis replied, "The baboons killed my son, Gaunu-tsaxau. I went to them as they were playing ball with his eye. I went to play ball with them. Then my son's eye vanished. The baboons said that I had it, and we fought over it. The baboons were fighting me, and I was fighting them. Then I flew away." But he did not mention that he had put his son's eye in the water.

Then the Mantis went to look at the place where he had put the child's eye into the water. He approached gently, so that he would not make a rustling noise. He saw that the eye had grown into a little child. The child knew that the Mantis was there, because he had heard him coming from a long way off. The child jumped up and splashed into the water. The Mantis laughed, because he was so delighted to see his son.

The child grew. It became like what it had been before. But it did not recognize the Mantis.

The child lay in the sun on the bank. The Mantis came up to the child and caught hold of him. He anointed the child with his scent. He said, "Why are you afraid of me? I am your father, I who am the Mantis. I am here. You are my son. You are Gaunu-tsaxau. I am the Mantis, I whose son you are." And he took the child home.

The Story of the Leopard Tortoise

The people had gone hunting. One of them, a woman, was ill. She perceived a man who came up to her hut; he had been hunting, and he came to see whether she was all right.

She asked the man to rub her neck with fat, for it ached. The man rubbed it with fat for her. The woman's neck swallowed his hands. It held his hands tight. The man's hands decayed away inside her neck.

Soon she saw another man, who returned from hunting. She said to him, "Rub me with fat a little."

The man whose hands had decayed away in her neck was hiding his hands, so that the other man would not see how badly he was hurt. He said, "Yes, my friend, rub our elder sister with a little fat, for she has been lying ill for a whole moon. Rub our elder sister with fat." He was hiding his hands the whole time.

The woman, who was really the Leopard Tortoise, said, "Rub my neck with fat." And the man took a little fat and rubbed it into the Leopard Tortoise's neck. The Leopard Tortoise drew in her head inside her shell, while his hands were still on her neck. The man's hands sank into her neck. He threw the Leopard Tortoise on the ground, trying to crack her shell, but the Leopard Tortoise held him fast.

The other man had taken out his hands from behind his back. He said, "Feel what I have had to feel!" and he showed the other one his hands. Then he left. The other man continued to dash the Leopard Tortoise upon the ground.

When the first man arrived home, his people exclaimed, "Where have you been?" He answered that his hands had been swallowed up inside the Leopard Tortoise's neck, and that was why he had not returned home sooner. The people said, "Are you a fool? Did your parents not tell you? The Leopard Tortoise always appears to be dead, but that is just so she can trick us. She is always deceiving us."

The Hyena's Revenge

One day the Hyena went to the Lion's house. The Lion ate but did not share. He was stingy with some quagga's flesh that he had caught. The Hyena looked hungrily on but did not say anything. He decided that he would play a trick on the Lion.

The next day the Lion came to the Hyena's house. The Hyena was boiling some ostrich flesh in a pot.

"That smells good," the Lion said.

"Would you like some ostrich soup?" the Hyena asked.

The Hyena handed the pot to the Lion. The Lion took hold of the pot, while the pot was hot, singeing his paws. The Hyena grasped the pot with a cloth and said, "O Lion! Allow me to pour soup into your mouth." The Hyena poured burning hot soup into the Lion's mouth. Then he put the pot on the Lion's head. The hot pot burned the Lion's head. The hot soup dripped down and burned the Lion's eyes, just as it had burned the inside of his mouth. He died, his head inside the pot and his innards scalded.

The Hyena took up his stick and beat the Lion. The Hyena beat the Lion so hard that the pot split in two.

The Hyena killed the Lion with hot soup. He intended to burn the Lion to death, and he did so, just because the Lion had been miserly with some quagga's flesh. He lured the Lion with ostrich flesh, knowing that the Lion would not be able to resist that temptation.

The lion marries a lioness because the lion is a male lion. The hyena marries a female hyena because the hyena is a male hyena. The leopard marries a leopardess because the leopard is a male leopard. The lion is jealous with his food because he is a lion. This is just the way things are.

Ostriches (male, female, young ones)

Kwǎ-kkwǎra gwāi.
Male.

Otis afra, Lin

Kwǎ-kkwǎra lǎityi.
Female.

Diä!kwǎin, March, 1875.

The Lion Jealous of the Voice of the Ostrich

The male Lions one day conspired to deceive the Ostrich. They were jealous, because the Lion women were always going around saying that the Ostrich had a beautiful voice, and they never complimented the male Lions for how fine and strong their voices were. They praised only the Ostrich.

The male Lions stood talking. One of them said, "What are we going to do about this? I can't stand all the attention the Ostrich is getting from our women."

Another Lion said, "We must tell the women to make a game of 'gebbi-ggu, as the Bushmen do. You know that game, don't you? The women sing like Ostriches, and the men sing like Ostriches in reply. Let's get the women to play this game, and we'll see if it's the Ostrich himself that they admire so much, or just his voice."

Another Lion spoke, saying, "How can it be that the Ostrich calls so sweetly?"

And the other Lion answered, "The Ostrich calls with his lungs. His throat sounds a little, but his call really lies deep down in his chest. You call with your mouth. It doesn't sound very strong when you do that. The Ostrich's call is much nicer."

The other Lion answered, saying, "Well, let's make a game of 'gebbi-ggu. We'll lure an Ostrich that way, and then we can take out his lungs and eat them. Then we'll be able to call out loudly, sounding just like the Ostrich, after we have eaten the Ostrich's lungs."

And the Lions spoke. Then they said to the women, "Let's make a game of *'gebbi-ggu.'"* They wanted to listen to learn whether the women admired the Ostrich, or merely his call.

The women made a game of *'gebbi-ggu.* They called out like Ostriches, and the male Lions called back like Ostriches in reply. The Ostrich was hiding in his house.

The Lions called, but their voices were thin. The Lion women did not applaud them, for they felt that the Lions did not call well.

The Ostrich, attracted by all the calling, came. He called out from afar. And the Lion women exclaimed, "I wish that the Lion sang as well as the Ostrich. Our men sound as if they had put their tails into their mouths, but the Ostrich calls beautifully."

The male Lions looked at each other and said, "Do you see that? Our women are acting as if they loved the Ostrich. They love him, and not just his call. He possesses a sweet call, that's true, but the women really love him alone."

The male Lions grew angry because the Lion women loved the Ostrich. The Lions ran up to the Ostrich. One of them grabbed the Ostrich by its throat. He scratched the Ostrich's throat; he scratched, tearing it. And he called out, "Let's see how sweetly you call now!" as he kicked and scratched and clawed at the Ostrich's throat.

The Ostrich whirled around and kicked at the Lion, tearing his throat. The Ostrich said, "This Lion is angry with me, because he sounds like he holds his tail in his mouth when he calls. This is why the Lion women do not praise him. The women feel that he does not call nicely. He does not sound like me. If he did, then the Lion women would have praised him." And the Ostrich ran away.

Therefore, we should also do as the Lion attempted to do. If he had killed the Lion, he would have eaten the Ostrich's lungs so that he might sound like the Ostrich.

This is why our grandfathers gave us the Ostrich's lungs to eat, so that we might also resemble the Ostrich. We asked them whether we should bake the Ostrich's lungs, and they said, no, we should eat them raw. For if we were to eat the Ostrich's lungs when they were cooked, we would not sound like the Ostrich. They also said that we should not chew the Ostrich's lungs, but instead that we should swallow them down whole. For if we chewed the Ostrich's lungs, we would not sound like the Ostrich.

Our grandfathers said: "Come over here and let me give you some of this Ostrich's lungs." And we answered, "O grandfathers! We do not want to eat the Ostrich's lungs. They're raw!" And our grandfathers said, if we ate them raw, we would resemble the Lion, who was once so angry about the Ostrich's fine calling. Our grandfathers said that we would also be angry with our friends if they had sweet voices and earned praise from the women; we would be jealous and fight with our friends if the women did not applaud us, too.

The Resurrection of the Ostrich

A Bushman killed an Ostrich that was protecting its eggs. He carried away the Ostrich to the house. And his wife took off the Ostrich's short feathers, which were inside the net, because they were bloody. They put the feathers outside on some bushes. They ate the Ostrich's meat.

A little whirlwind came to them. It blew the Ostrich feathers around. A little Ostrich feather had some blood on it. It sailed far up into sky and then fell down, whirling, whirling, into a pool of water. It got wet.

After a while the feather became conscious.

It became Ostrich flesh. It grew feathers. It grew wings. It grew legs.

It walked out of the water and basked in the sun at the water's edge. Its feathers were black, for he was a little male Ostrich. He dried his feathers on the water's bank. Then he walked away, unstiffening his legs. He walked on, strengthening his feet, making his feet into the strong shoes that the Ostrich wears so that he never gets tired of walking around in the bush. He lay down, hardening his breastbone in the sun. He walked away, eating tender young bushes. He swallowed small young plants, just as a little Ostrich does.

His little feather became the Ostrich. The wind, the little whirlwind, blew it up into the sky.

The Ostrich thought of the places where he scratched the ground before he was killed. He let himself grow. Then he went to his old house, where he once died.

36

He went to fetch his wives. He had two of them, but because he had died, he added another she Ostrich to his family. He married three Ostrich wives.

His breastbone was bone. He roared, hardening his ribs, making his ribs into bone.

Then he scratched out another house.

Roaring, he called his wives. They came running to him, and they ran around and around together, admiring each other.

When he had strengthened his flesh, the Ostrich felt heavy, because his legs were big, his knees were large; he had grown large feathers, and not the downy quills he had when he was a young Ostrich. The quills had become great feathers, and those feathers had become strong, old feathers.

He roared strongly, for his ribs were big.

He was a grownup Ostrich. His wing feathers were long.

He scratched the earth, so that the females could lay eggs, for his claws were hard and made to scratch. He brought the females to his new house. The females stood there eating.

He went back outside and scratched some more. He scratched gritty sand on the house, because it was damp, so that he could make it dry.

The she-Ostriches looked at the house, admiring it. One she-Ostrich lay down to try the house. She thought it was nice, but she wanted to sleep outside, because the inside of the house was still wet, as if the rain had newly fallen. Even so, she lay there inside, making the ground soft and dry, so that another female could come and lay an egg in a dry, warm place.

The Ostrich galloped around and around, driving the females inside the house. They entered, scratching and pecking. Flapping their wings, they pecked at the eggs they had laid. They lay more eggs, and they drove the male out of the house, for a man's place is outside, protecting the eggs.

37

The Ostrich, for this reason, drives away the jackal, which comes looking to steal the Ostrich's eggs. He drives away the jackal, so that the jackal may not kill his children. He kicks at the jackal with his big feet.

The Vultures, Their Elder Sister, and Her Husband

Once the Vultures declared that they were going to make a woman their elder sister. They did, and then they came to live with her.

When their elder sister's husband brought home a springbok, they ate it up in an instant, greedily. And their elder sister's husband cursed them. He scolded them, because they did not save any of the springbok for him.

Their elder sister took the springbok's skin. She singed it. Their elder sister boiled the skin of the springbok. She took it out of the pot.

And they all took hold of the pieces of skin and swallowed them down. Their elder sister's husband scolded them again, because they had just finished eating the body of the springbok, but still they ate again.

The Vultures were afraid of their elder sister's husband. They flapped away, flying off in all directions. They sat down on tree branches and skulked around, casting furtive looks at their elder sister's husband.

Their elder sister's husband went hunting. He again went and killed a springbok. He brought the springbok home, slung upon his back.

The Vultures swooped down. They came and ate up the springbok in a flash.

Their elder sister's husband scolded them. They moved away, flapping their wings loudly, and sat down on tree branches.

Their elder sister singed the springbok's skin. She boiled the springbok's skin. Their elder sister gave the Vultures pieces of the skin, and they swallowed them down.

The next day their elder sister's husband said that his wife had to go with him when he went to hunt. If he caught anything, he said, then they would eat what he killed right there on the spot, on the hunting ground, for his younger sisters-in-law were now in the habit of eating up the springbok without saving any of the meat for him. Therefore, he said, the wife should go with him.

The wife went with him.

The Vultures, when their elder sister and her husband had gone, went into their house to look for food. When they did not find anything to eat, they sat down in the trees outside the house, conspiring about it.

One said, "You there, you ascend, and then come and tell us where our elder sister has gone off to."

And another said, "Let our youngest sister be the one to ascend. Then she must tell us what she sees."

A Vulture who was a little Vulture girl arose from her seat. She ascended.

The other Vultures said, "Let's see what our little sister will do."

The little Vulture went off, disappearing in the sky far away, so high that her sisters could no longer see her.

The Vultures sat for a long time. They waited. And after a long time their younger sister fell from out of the sky above. She came and sat among them.

And they exclaimed, "What is the place like, the place where our elder sister has gone to?"

And their younger sister said, "You should go have a look for yourselves. It would be better than if I tried to tell you about it."

Another Vulture, who was a grownup girl, arose. She ascended. She went off, disappearing in the sky. And then, after a while, she descended from above. She sat in the trees with the other vultures.

And the other Vultures said, "Well, what is the place like?"

The Vulture sister said, "There is nothing the matter with the place. The place is very beautiful. I can see the whole place, all the trunks and branches of all the trees. It seems to be just the sort of place where we would find a springbok, for it is full of trees under which a springbok can rest. It is full of trees, and very beautiful."

They all arose, all of them, and they ascended into the sky. They wanted their elder sister to get something for them to eat. They were afraid of her husband, but not so afraid that they stayed away.

They arrived. They found a springbok themselves, and they killed it. Then they saw their elder sister coming along with her husband.

They ate in great haste. They squawked at each other, saying: "You must eat! You must eat! You must eat quickly! For that accursed man who comes cannot stand us!"

They finished gulping down the springbok. They flew heavily away. Their elder sister's husband came along, but all that was left for him to pick up were a few bones.

The Vultures saw another springbok. They descended and killed the springbok. They began to devour it.

Their elder sister saw them and followed them. Her husband was not with her.

The Vultures saw her coming. They ate, they ate, they ate. They looked around. They ate up all the flesh. Then they said, "We really ought to leave something for our elder sister. Let's leave the undercut for her. Let's leave her a really good piece of meat."

But they continued eating all the same. They ate up all of the springbok, saving only the skin.

"Oh, well," they said. "Maybe there's some meat left on the inside of the skin."

When their elder sister came near, they flew away in all directions, ashamed at their gluttony.

Their elder sister said, "How can you do this to me? I have been giving you food all this time. You act as if I had been the one who scolded you!"

And their elder sister came up to the springbok skin and grabbed it away from them. She returned home and chewed unhappily on little pieces of boiled skin.

The Vultures went flying away, seeking another springbok, just as they always do today.

The Stone Man, the Lioness, and the Children

There was once a pool of water to which a Lioness would come to drink. She was an old Lioness, and she was lame. Because of that, she could not hunt, so she had gone into the Bushmen village in the valley below the pool and gathered up the children. The Bushmen children would do her hunting for her.

A stone man came to this pool. He drank. Sniffing around, he sensed that children were nearby.

He went to the Lioness's house. The Lioness was not at home. She was at the pool, dipping up water.

The stone man went to the children. The stone man sat down. And the stone man said, "O children sitting here by the Lioness's fire! The fire of your people is down in that ravine over there." Two children arose. They went away to their own people.

And the stone man said again, "O children sitting here by the Lioness's fire! The fire of your people is down in that ravine over there." Three children arose. They went away to their own people.

And the stone man said again, "O children sitting here by the Lioness's fire! The fire of your people is down in that ravine over there." One child arose. She went away to her own people.

And the stone man said again, "O children sitting here by the Lioness's fire! The fire of your people is down in that ravine over there." Two children arose. They went away to their own people.

And the stone man said again, "O children sitting here by the Lioness's fire! The fire of your people is down in that ravine over there." Two children arose. They went away to their own people.

And the stone man said again, "O children sitting here by the Lioness's fire! The fire of your people is down in that ravine over there." Three children arose. They went away to their own people.

And the stone man said again, "O children sitting here by the Lioness's fire! The fire of your people is down in that ravine over there." Two children arose. They went away to their own people. There were no more children left after that.

The stone man sat waiting for the Lioness.

The Lioness came back from the pool. She came along looking at her house. She did not see the children. And she stammered with rage, "Why do the children children children children, the children not sit by my fire? Why do the children not play here, as they used to? It must have something to do with this man who sits outside my house. His head is made of stone."

And she became angry about it, when she saw the stone man. She exclaimed, "The stone man sits here!" She walked up to the house. She exclaimed, "Where are my children?"

And the stone man said: "Your children they are not."

And the Lioness exclaimed, "Go away! Give me back my children!"

The stone man said, "Your children they were not."

And the Lioness caught hold of his head. She growled, "*xabbabbu*," gnawing at the stone man's head. Then she exclaimed, "Oh! Oh dear! Oh dear! Oh dear! Oh dear! My teeth!"

The stone man said again, "I told you that they were not your children."

The Lioness exclaimed, "You have brought my destruction!"

The stone man repeated, "Your children they were not. They were not my children. They are the children of the human beings, and not of us."

And the stone man arose. He returned home.

The Lioness sat in anger outside her house. She was angry because the stone man had come and taken away the children from her. They had been living peacefully with her, and she felt that she had been kind to them. She even loved them, but the stone man came and broke her heart.

The Mason Wasp and His Wife

The Mason Wasp once was walking along. His wife walked behind him. The wife said, "O my husband! Shoot that hare for me!"

The Mason Wasp set down his quiver and unslung his bow from his back. He said, "Where is the hare?"

His wife said, "The hare is over there, lying underneath that bush."

The Mason Wasp rummaged through his quiver to select an arrow. He was slow about it.

His wife said, "Put down your quiver! Why are you taking so long?"

The Mason Wasp put down his quiver.

His wife said, "Why are you like this? If you had put down your quiver and sent an arrow flying, we would now be eating hare."

The Mason Wasp walked, turning to one side. He aimed at his wife. He shot, hitting her breastbone with a sharp arrow. And his wife fell down dead.

Then the Mason Wasp exclaimed, *"Yi yi hihi!* O my wife *hi!"* as if he had not been the one to shoot his wife.

But he did. He cried, but he shot his wife, and she died.

The Frog's Story

A girl lay ill. She was lying down. She did not eat the food her mother gave her. She lay ill.

She killed the children of the water; they were what she ate. Her mother did not know that she had killed the water's children, that they were what she ate. She would not eat what her mother gave to her.

Her mother was there. They went out to look for ant eggs. The mother spoke, ordering the girl's sister to remain at home. The old woman said that she must look at the things that her elder sister ate.

They left the child at home, and they went out to seek ant eggs. They intended for the child to look at the things that her elder sister ate.

The elder sister went out from the house of illness and descended to the spring, as she intended to kill another water-child. Her sister was in the hut. She went and killed a water-child, and she carried the water-child home. Her sister looked on as she boiled the water-child's flesh; and she ate it; and she lay down; and she again went to lie down. Her sister looked on as she did all this.

Their mother returned. The younger child told her mother about it; for her elder sister had gone to kill a handsome thing at the water.

Their mother said: "It is a water-child!"

But their mother did not speak about it after that. Instead, she again went out to look for ant eggs.

And when she was seeking about for food, the clouds came up. And she spoke, she said, "Something is not right at home; for a whirlwind is bringing things to the spring. For something is not going on well at home. Therefore, the whirlwind is taking things away to the spring." Because her daughter killed the water's children, the whirlwind took them away to the spring. Something had not gone well at home, for her daughter had been killing the water's children. That was why the whirlwind took them away to the spring, because she had killed the water's children.

The older girl was the one who first went into the spring, and then she became a frog. Her sister became a frog. Her mother went into the spring, following the whirlwind. Her daughters were frogs. Their mother also became a frog. The whirlwind brought them all to the spring. Her daughter was already in the spring. She was a frog.

Her father also came to become a frog, for the whirlwind brought her father – who had been at a hunting ground far away – to the spring, to the place where his daughter was. Her father's arrows grew into reeds out by the spring, for the great whirlwind had brought them to the spring. He also became a frog. Likewise his wife, she also became a frog. That whole family became frogs, and all because one of them ate the water's children.

The *Narru* and Her Husband

A man of the early race married a *narru* bird, the little bird whose plumage looks like that of an ostrich. The *narru* put dusty ant eggs into a bag after her husband had dug them out of the ground. She went to wash the ant eggs. Then they returned home.

They went out the next day to seek more food, she and her husband. The husband dug out ant eggs; he put the ant eggs into his leather bag. And the husband again dug out other ant eggs. He again arose and found other ant eggs. He dug them out from the earth. The bag became full.

They arose the next day, and the husband dug out other ant eggs. He found other ant eggs; he dug them out, he dug them out. And he exclaimed, "Give me your little bag so that I may fill it with ant eggs."

And the wife said, "We are not accustomed to putting dirty ant eggs into our bag, we who are of the house of *narru*."

And he exclaimed, "Give me, give me your little bag so that I may fill it up with ant eggs."

And the wife said: "You should put the ant eggs back into the ground, for we are not accustomed to putting dirty ant eggs into our bag."

And he exclaimed, "Give me, give me your little bag so that I may fill it up with ant eggs."

And the wife exclaimed, "You should put the ant eggs back into the ground and cover them up with dirt."

And he exclaimed, "Give me your bag!" And he snatched the bag away. His wife's entrails were inside the bag, and they poured down.

And he, crying, exclaimed, "Oh dear! Oh my wife! What shall I do?"

The wife sang,

> *We, who are of the house of narru,*
> *We are not used to putting earthy ant eggs*
> *Into our bag;*
> *We, who are of the house of narru,*
> *We are not used to putting earthy ant eggs*
> *Into our bag.*

while she walked on replacing her entrails. She sang:

> *We, who are of the house of narru,*
> *We are not used to putting earthy ant eggs*
> *Into our bag.*

Her mother, sitting in a tree, heard her song. She exclaimed to her other children, "Go find the place where your elder sister went to seek food, for the noise of the wind sounds like her song. I think that her husband is not treating her well. The noise of the wind sounds like a person, singing windward."

And her children stood up and flew away. They came back and said, "Your daughter comes, falling down on the path."

Then the mother said, "See for yourself! This is how human husbands behave. They do mad things, for they do not understand. They marry us as if they understood anything at all about us.

Then she ran to meet her daughter. She went to put the little leather bag upon her daughter. Holding up her daughter's entrails, she bound her daughter with bandages. She slowly took her daughter home to her hut.

She was angry about what had happened to her daughter. When her daughter's husband wanted to come to visit his wife, she was angry. Her daughter's husband went back to his own people, for his mother-in-law had driven him away. She said that her daughter's husband should go back to his people, for none of them understood the ways of the birds. Therefore, her daughter's husband went back, and the *narru* wife continued to dwell there with her mother. Thus it is that humans and birds do not live in each other's houses today.

The Young Man of the Ancient Race
Who Was Carried off by a Lion

A young man was out hunting. He ascended a hill. While he sat on the crest looking around for game, he became sleepy. And he thought that he would lie down, for he was very sleepy. What could have happened to him? He had not felt like this before.

He lay down and slept.

A lion came. It went to a pool of water there on the crest, because the noonday heat had made it thirsty. The lion saw the man lying asleep, and it grabbed him up and took him away.

The man awoke, startled. He saw that it was a lion that had taken him up.

He decided to stay still, for the lion would kill him with a single bite if he stirred. He decided to see what the lion intended to do, for the lion appeared to think that he was dead.

The lion carried him to a wormbush tree and laid him in its branches.

The lion thought that it would not be able to slake its thirst if it ate the man right away. The lion decided to first go to the water and drink its fill, so that it could eat the man afterward without being thirsty.

The lion trod on the man, pressing his head between the branches of the wormbush tree. Then it stepped back away from the tree.

The man turned his head a little.

The lion saw this and thought, why had the man's head moved? The lion thought that perhaps it had not put the man away in the tree carefully enough. So it again trod on the man, pressing his head into the middle of the branches of the wormbush tree. And then it licked the man's tears.

The man had cried, and so the lion licked his eyes. A stick was poking into the back of the man's neck, right there in the little hollow at the back of his head.

The man turned his head a little, looking steadfastly at the lion. He turned his head just a little bit, to move away from the stick that was poking so sharply.

The lion looked to see why it was that the man had moved again. And it licked the man's tears. It stepped on the man again, thoroughly pressing down the man's head, sure that this time the man would be tucked away inside the tree and would not move.

The man sensed that by now the lion was thinking that he was not really dead. This time he did not stir, although the stick was still piercing him.

The lion saw that it appeared as if it had put the man away nicely, for the man did not stir. The lion went a few steps away and looked back at the man. The man peeked out through his eyelashes. He saw what the lion was doing.

The lion went away, ascending the hill. The lion descended the hill on the other side, while the man gently turned his head to see whether the lion had really gone. He saw that the lion stood peeping behind the top of the hill, because the lion thought that it seemed as if the man were alive.

The lion saw that the man was lying still. He decided to run to the water and get a drink. Then he would come back and eat the man. By this time it was very hungry. It was very thirsty, and very, very hungry.

The man lay looking at the lion. He waited. The man saw

that the lion had disappeared. It seemed as if it had gone away. But the man waited. He thought that he would lie still, to see whether the lion would come peeping over the hill. For the lion is a cunning thing. It might, the man thought, try to deceive him, acting as if it had really gone away.

The man waited while the lion peeped over the hill, then crept away, then pepped over the hill, then crept away again.

Finally, the man saw that a long time had passed since the lion had peeped over the hill at him.

He did not arise and go running away. He arose slowly, and the first thing he did then was to spring to a different place nearby. He did not want the lion to know where he had gone. Then he ran in a zigzag direction up and down the hill, hoping that the lion would not be able to smell out his footsteps. He knew that the lion would come back and then start looking for him. His people knew that the lion never abandons an animal that it has killed. It does not leave it uneaten.

When he came down to the bottom of the hill, he called out to the people at home, saying that he had just been stolen away by a lion while the sun stood high. He had been carried off, he yelled.

The young man told his people to gather up some hartebeest skins and wrap him up in them. He thought that the lion would come looking for him. His people knew that the lion would never abandon its prey.

Therefore, he called, his people should hide him from the lion.

And so the people did. The people rolled him up in reed mats and hartebeest skins. They wanted to be sure that he was well hidden when the lion came looking for him.

Then the people went out to look for *koeisse*, an edible root. They dug out *koeisse* and brought it home, and they baked it.

An old Bushman was going along gathering wood for his wife, so that his wife could make a fire and bake her *koeisse*.

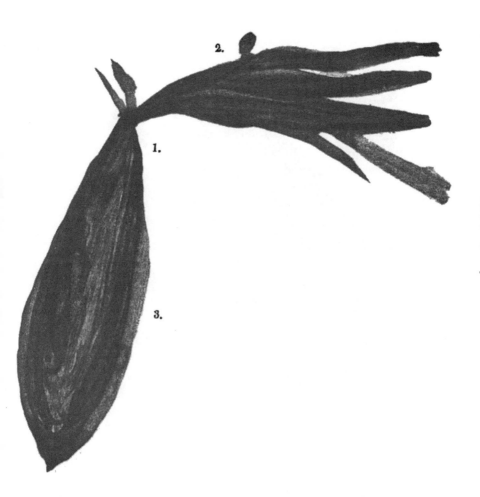

1. ǁhúru.

A ground-plant, with a white flower (2), which smells badly.

3.

The root is very large, and is sometimes used as a cooking-pot by the !kuń, in the absence of a pot. It is eaten by elephants and the ǁniń (the eland), but not by the !kuń.

The plant climbs or lies on the
ground ; it has long branches
and a small white flower.

!goṅ‖ná, a root eaten by the !kuṅ generally, as food.
(It appears also to be eaten as the *sole* food of those who have shot an eland, until
the animal is dead.) *Tamme. June 11th. 1881*

He saw the lion as it came over the top of the hill, just at the spot where the young man had descended. He saw that the lion was following the man's tracks. He called out that the lion was coming over the crest of the hill.

The young man's mother said, "You must not allow the lion to come into our huts. You must shoot it dead before it gets here."

And the people slung on their quivers and went out to meet the lion. They were shooting at the lion. They shot and shot, but the lion would not die.

An old woman said, "You must give the lion a child. Then the lion will go away from us."

The lion answered with a roar. It said that it did not want a child. It wanted the young man whose tears it had licked. He was the one it wanted.

The other people said, "In what way were you shooting the lion that you could not manage to kill it?"

And an old man said, "Can you not see that the lion must be sorcerer? It will not die when we are shooting at it. It insists on having the man whom it carried off."

The people threw children to the lion. But the lion had no interest in them. The lion did not want the children. It sniffed at them but left them alone.

The people were shooting at the lion while it sought the man. The people were shooting at it. The people said, "We must get assegais. We must kill that lion."

The people were shooting at it. But it seemed as if they were doing nothing, for the lion did not die. They were stabbing it with assegais. They tried to stab it to death. But it seemed as if they were doing nothing, for the lion did not die.

The lion continued to look for the young man. It said that it wanted the young man whose tears it had licked. He was the one it wanted.

It tore the people's huts apart. It scratched them. It tore the huts to pieces.

And the people said, "Can you not see that the lion will not eat the children we have given to it?"

And the people said, "Can you not see that it must be a sorcerer?"

And the people said, "We must give a little girl to the lion. Maybe the lion will eat her. Maybe then it will go away."

But the lion did not want the girl. The lion wanted only the man whom it had carried of. He was the one it wanted.

And the people said that they did not know what else to do. It had been midday when they first started shooting at the lion, and the lion would not die. Now it was sunset. "We do not know what to do," they said. "The lion has refused the children. It has refused the little girl. It is destroying our huts."

And the people said, "Say to the young man's mother that she must, even though she loves the young man, she must take him out of the hartebeest skins, she must give the young man to the lion, even though he is the child of her heart. She can see that the sun is about to set, and the lion is still threatening us. The lion will not go and leave us alone. It insists on having the young man."

And the young man's mother said, "You may give my child to the lion. You must not allow the lion to eat my child, however. You must kill the lion."

And the people, when the young man's mother had spoken, the people took the young man out from the hartebeest skins in which they had rolled him up. They gave the young man to death.

The lion bit the young man. As it was biting the young man, the people were shooting at it. The people were stabbing it. The lion bit the young man to death.

And the lion spoke. It said to the people that this time it would die. It had got hold of the man it had been seeking. It had got hold of him and killed him!

And it died, while the man also lay dead. The lion also lay dead, beside the man.

Sun, Moon, and Stars

The Children Are Sent to Throw
the Sleeping Sun into the Sky

Once some children went to lift up the Sun, while the Sun lay sleeping. They approached him gently, mindful of an old woman's instructions. She said that they should catch the Sun and throw him up there into the sky, so that the ant eggs might become dry for them, so that the Sun might make the whole place bright, so that the Sun could make all places bright as it went along in the sky.

She said, "O children! You must wait for the Sun to down to sleep. We are cold. While he lies asleep, gently approach, and lift him up, all of you together, and throw him up into the sky."

The old woman also said, "You must sit down when you get there, and wait for a while. See whether the Sun is awake. See whether the Sun is looking at you. Wait for a while. Be patient, and then catch him when he sleeps."

The children sat down and waited. The Sun lay down. He lifted up his elbow, and his armpit shone upon the ground as he lay there. After a while the Sun fell asleep. The children caught him and lifted him up, all together. They threw him up into the sky, just as the old woman had told them to do.

The old woman said to the children, "O children! You must tell him to move through the sky, tell him to move forward, so that he becomes hot as he passes. That way the ant eggs will dry so that we can eat them."

The children called up to the Sun, saying, "O grandfather, O Sun! Become hot, so that the ant eggs may dry for us. Become hot, so that you can give light to the whole earth, so that the whole earth may become warm in the summer. Shine, taking away the darkness. As you go, the darkness will go away."

The Sun comes, and the darkness goes away. The Sun comes, the Sun sets; the darkness comes, the Moon comes at night. The day breaks, the Sun comes out, the darkness goes away. The Moon comes out, the Moon brightens the darkness, the darkness departs; the Moon comes out, the Moon shines, taking away the darkness; it goes along, it has made bright the darkness, it sets. The Sun comes out, the Sun chases away the darkness. The Sun takes away the Moon, the Sun pierces it with his knife, and the Moon it decays away. The Moon calls out, "O Sun! Leave my backbone for the children!" And the Sun does so. The Moon painfully goes away, he painfully returns home, he painfully goes along. He goes on to become another Moon, which is whole, because his backbone remains. He lives again, although he was so near to death. He becomes a new Moon. He puts on another stomach and becomes large. He walks in the night.

The Sun is here, all the earth is bright. The Sun is here, and the people walk while the place is light, while the earth is light. The people perceive the bushes, they see the other people. They see the meat they are eating. They also see the springbok, and they chase the springbok in summer; they also chase the ostrich while the Sun shines; they also steal up to the gemsbok; they also steal up to the kudu, while the whole place is bright. They also visit each other, while the Sun shines, while the earth is bright, while the Sun shines upon the path. They also travel in summer; they shoot in summer; they hunt in summer; they see the springbok in summer; they go round to chase the springbok; they lie down in their little houses of brush, and the springbok come.

Variant

The Sun was once a man, but not one of the early race of people who preceded the First Bushmen in their country. He gave forth brightness only for a space around his own dwelling. Some children stole up to him and threw him into the sky. Before the children threw him up, he had not been in the sky, but had lived at his own house on earth. Because his shining had been confined to a certain space around his own dwelling, the rest of the country seemed as if the sky were very cloudy, as it looks now, when the Sun is behind thick clouds. The sky was black. The shining came from one of the Sun's armpits, as he lay with one arm lifted up. When he put down his arm, darkness fell everywhere; when he lifted it up again, it was as if day came. In the day, the Sun's light used to be white; but, at night, it was red, like a fire. When the Sun was thrown up into the sky it became round, and it was never a man again.

A Bushman Woman with Digging-Stick
(Photographed at Salt River in 1884)

The Wife of the Dawn's Heart Star

They sought grubs, they were digging out grubs. They went about, sifting grubs, digging out grubs. And when the grub larvae tried to go into the earth, underneath that little hill over there, they gathered them. They sifted the grub larvae on the hunting ground.

The Hyena took the blackened perspiration of her armpits, and she put it into the grub larvae. And she this gave to Lynx, the wife of Jupiter, the Dawn's Heart Star. And Lynx exclaimed, she said to her younger sister, "Leave these larvae alone. I will be the one who eats them. You are the one who will take care of my child. This food, its smell is not nice."

As Lynx sat, eating the grubs, her ornaments – her earrings, bracelets, leglets, and anklets – came off by themselves. Her skin cloak also loosened itself and slid off. Her skin petticoat also loosened itself and slid off. Her shoes also loosened themselves.

Lynx sprang up and trotted away, naked. Her younger sister, shrieking, followed her. Lynx went into the reeds by the pool. She went to sit in the reeds.

Her younger sister exclaimed, "O Lynx! Will you abandon your child? Will you not first allow him to suckle?" And Lynx said: "Bring him to me, and I will nurse him. I want to talk with you anyway, while my mind is still clear."

Lynx spoke. She said to her younger sister, "You must be quick about bringing my child to me, while I am still conscious. Bring the child tomorrow morning."

Her younger sister returned home. The Hyena followed her. The Hyena had put on Lynx's ornaments. They returned home while the Dawn's Heart and the rest were still out hunting.

The Dawn's Heart returned home. The child was crying, and his wife's younger sister was trying to console him.

He came. He exclaimed, "Why is it that Lynx is not attending to the child while the child cries there?"

The Hyena did not speak. Lynx's younger sister was soothing the child. She waited. Her elder sister's husband again went out to hunt. Lynx's younger sister took the child upon her back. She went to her elder sister. She walked, arriving at the reeds. She exclaimed, "O Lynx! Let the child suckle."

And Lynx sprang out of the reeds, Lynx came running, Lynx caught hold of her.

Lynx's younger sister turned her body to one side and gave her elder sister the child. She said, "I am here!"

And Lynx allowed the child to suckle. She said, "You must bring the child again tomorrow, while I am still conscious. I feel as if my thinking-strings are about to fall down."

And her younger sister took the child upon her back and returned home, while Lynx went back into the reeds.

Near sunset, the younger sister went to Lynx. She was worried about her sister. Lynx had said, as she was walking into the reeds, "You must quickly bring the child, for I feel as if I am about to forget you. I barely know who you are."

So her younger sister took the child near sunset. She went to her elder sister. She stood by the pool. She exclaimed, "O Lynx! Let the child suckle."

Her elder sister sprang out of the reeds. She ran up to her younger sister. Her younger sister said, "I am here! I am here!"

Lynx allowed the child to suckle. She said, "You must quickly come again, for I feel as if I am about to forget you. I can no longer think of who you are."

Bushman Dancing-Rattles

Her younger sister returned home, while Lynx went back into the reeds.

The next morning her younger sister went to her elder sister. She walked, coming, coming, coming, coming. She stood by the pool. And she exclaimed, "O Lynx! Let the child suckle."

And her elder sister sprang out of the reeds, she ran up to her younger sister, she caught hold of her younger sister. Her younger sister, springing aside, gave her the child. Her younger sister said, "I am here!"

Lynx spoke. She said to her younger sister, "You must not continue to come to me. I no longer feel that I know you."

And her younger sister returned home.

And they went to make a ceremonial dance there at the hut. They played. The men played with them while the women clapped their hands. The men nodded their heads while the women clapped their hands for them. Then the Dawn's Heart, nodding his head, went up to his younger sister-in-law. He put his hand on his younger sister-in-law's shoulder.

His younger sister-in-law swerved aside. She exclaimed, "Leave me alone! Your wives, the old she-hyenas, may clap their hands for you." She pointed to the Hyena. The Dawn's Heart had not noticed her before.

Then the Dawn's Heart ran to the Hyena, who was crouching in the shadows inside the hut. He took aim with his assegai. He pierced the place where the Hyena had been sitting. The Hyena sprang out. She ran, burning herself in the fire as she sprang away. This is why hyenas walk with a limp, because that Hyena burned her feet in the fire.

Lynx's ornaments remained at the place where the Hyena had been sitting, where she had been wearing them. She sprang away, while the ornaments remained.

And the Dawn's Heart scolded his younger sister-in-law, asking why she had not told him that the Hyena had cast a spell on Lynx, why she had let the Hyena conceal herself in his hut. He demanded that his sister-in-law tell him where Lynx was.

His younger sister-in-law said, "You must wait for the place to become light. You seem to think that your wife is like she was before. We will go to see your wife when the sun has come out."

In the morning, the Dawn's Heart said that his younger sister-in-law must lead them to Lynx. Then his younger sister-in-law said, "We ought to take goats, so that your wife will have something to eat." Therefore, they drove some goats before them. They drove the goats, drove the goats. They took the goats to the reeds.

The younger sister told the Dawn's Heart to stand behind her. She stood beside the goats. Then she exclaimed, "O Lynx! Let the child suckle!"

Then her elder sister sprang out of the reeds. Lynx came running. When she had run to her younger sister, she saw the goats. She turned aside and caught hold of a goat.

Then the Dawn's Heart caught hold of his wife, who was busy grappling with the goat. His younger sister-in-law also caught hold of Lynx. Other people caught hold of her. Other people caught hold of the goats; they cut the goats open, they took out the contents of their stomachs, and they anointed Lynx with them. They rubbed the hair from her skin. Exhausted, Lynx sat down. She said, "You must leave the hair on the tips of my ears, for otherwise I won't be able to hear anything." And the Dawn's Heart left the hair on the tips of her ears.

From then on, the Dawn's Heart, when he was returning home, put an arrow on his bow, he walked, sticking the end of his assegai into the ground as he traveled along. His eyes were large as he came walking along. They resembled fires.

The people were afraid of him as he came, because of his eyes. They felt that his eyes resembled fires as he came walking along. The jackals were afraid of him. The Hyena was afraid of him. The Hyena is always afraid of the light.

The Origin of Death

When the Moon has newly returned alive, when another person has shown us the Moon, we look toward the place where the other has shown us the Moon, and when we look there we perceive the Moon, and when we perceive it we shut our eyes with our hands, and we exclaim, "O Moon yonder! Take my face! Give me your face! Take my face! It does not feel pleasant. Give me your face! When you have died, you return. When we think we will not see you again, you come. Give me your face, so that we may also return alive, when we die."

The hare was the one who said this, a long time ago. He spoke. He would not be silent. His mother had died, and he cried for her.

The Moon answered that the hare should stop crying, for his mother was not altogether dead. His mother would return to life.

The hare said that he has not willing to be silent. He knew that his mother would not come back. She was dead.

The Moon became angry because the hare had spoken to him in that way. He hit the hare with his fist, cleaving the hare's mouth, and as he hit the hare's mouth with his fist he exclaimed, "This person, his mouth will always be like this: he will always bear a scar on his mouth. When anyone approaches he will spring away. He will double up on his tracks and try to come back. The dogs will chase him. When they catch him, they will tear him to pieces, and he will die."

Our mothers used to say that the hare was once a man. And so the Moon cursed all humans while he made that one turn into a hare, with his split lip. Our mothers used to say that a little bit of the hare remains human, though, and that the hare has human flesh at its groin. Because of that, when we have killed a hare, we cut away that strip of flesh, which is really human flesh, from the time long ago when the hare was a man.

The hare should have said, "Yes, my mother is just sleeping for a little while. She will get up soon." If the hare had said this, we people would be like the Moon. We would only appear to die, but then we would return again. We would never die.

Do Not Look at the Moon
when Game Has Been Shot

We may not look at the Moon when we have shot game. Instead, we look down, lowering our heads, and not up toward the sky. For we are afraid of the Moon's shining. For, our mothers used to tell us, the Moon is not a good person, and he will hurt us if we look at him.

If we look at him when we have shot game, the beasts of prey will eat the game while the game lies dying. If the game does not die, it is because the Moon's water has fallen on it and caused it to live. For, our mothers used to tell us, the Moon's water, the water that glistens on the bush, resembles liquid honey. It falls on the game, and the game arises. The Moon's water cools the poison with which we shot the game; and the game arises, it goes on living, it shows no signs of the poison. The Moon's water cures it, and it lives. This is why animals do not fear the Moon

Therefore, our mothers said, we should not look at the things in the sky. Our mothers used to tell us that if we looked at the Moon, the game we shot would also go along like the Moon. Our mothers asked, did we not see the Moon's way of going across the sky? He was not in the habit of going to places that are near at hand; see how far away he is when the day breaks. The game would also do the same if we looked at the Moon. The day would break, and the game would still be going along, far away from us. If we followed the game it would take us away to a place where there was no water. We could die of thirst following the animals.

The Girl Who Made Stars

My mother told me that one time a girl arose from her place by the fire, put her hands into the wood ashes, and threw the ashes into the sky. She said to the ashes, "Wood ashes, you must become the Milky Way. You must lie white in the sky, and the stars will stand beside you." The ashes became the Milky Way. The Milky Way must go around with the stars, while the stars go to fetch the daybreak. The Milky Way stands still, and the stars sail along, following their own footprints.

The Milky Way comes to the place at which the girl threw up the wood ashes, and there it sets with the stars. The darkness comes out, and the stars grow red, where they had at first been white. When the stars are white, then the people go by night, when the ground has been made light, when the stars shine just a little. The Milky Way gently glows like embers in the fire. The girl said that the Milky Way should give a little light for the people, so that they could find their way home in the middle of the night. The earth would not have been light, had not the Milky Way been there, and the stars.

The Great Star Gaunu, Singing,
Names the Other Stars

Gaunu was once a great star. Once he sang out the other stars' names, for the felt that he was great among them and it was his right to give them their names. Because of him, the stars possess their names. He sang to some stars that are very small, naming them. He sang to some stars that are larger, naming them too.

The porcupine, when these stars have turned on their courses, will not remain on the hunting ground. He knows that it is dawn when Altair has turned back. He returns home, for he knows that they are the dawn's stars.

What the Stars Say

When the Bushmen are hungry, they ask the stars to take their hearts and give them their own. For a star is not small. It is large, as if it has just eaten. Therefore, they say, if the stars give them their hearts, the Bushmen will not go hungry.

The stars call out, *"Tsau! Tsau!"* The Bushmen say that the stars are cursing the springboks' eyes on the Bushmen's behalf. The stars say *"Tsau! Tsau!"* Summer is the time when they sound.

I would sit with my grandfather in the coolness outside, and he told me that the stars would curse the springboks' eyes for me.

My grandfather used to speak to Canopus, when Canopus had just come out. He said, "Give my your heart, for you sit in plenty. Give me your heart, and take mine, with which I am so desperately hungry. That way I might also be full, like you. I hunger, while you have so much food, for you are not small. Take my stomach and give me yours, so that you will know what it is like to be hungry. Give me your arm and take mine, for mine does not kill. I miss my aim." Then he would shut his mouth and sit down, sharpening his arrows.

Wind and Rain

The Child of the Wind

The son of the Wind had been lying still for a while, resting. But it wanted to play. He rolled a ball to a Bushmen boy called Nshnkati, saying, "O Nshnkati! There it goes!" And Nshnkati rolled the ball back to him, exclaiming, "O friend! There it goes!" Nshnkati did not know what the child of the Wind was called.

Nshnkati went to question his mother about the other one's name. He exclaimed: "O mother! Tell me the name of my friend there. We are playing ball, and he knows my name. I want to call him by his name."

His mother said, "O Nshnkati! I will not tell you your friend's name just now. That will have to wait. Your father must first make a sturdy shelter for us. After that I will tell you your friend's name. And when I have told you your friend's name, then you must promise me that if you call it out, then you will scamper away at once and run home. Otherwise the wind will blow you away."

His mother waited for a while. Then she said, "O Nshnkati, your friend's name is Izhrriten-kuan-kuan. He is also called Igau-Igaubu-ti. He is Izhrriten-kuan-kua; he is Igau-Igaubu-ti."

Nshnkati went to roll the ball back and forth with the son of the Wind. He did not utter his friend's name, though, because he remembered what his mother had said to him. He was afraid that the child of the Wind would blow him away to the ends of the earth.

Then Nshnkati saw that his father had sat down to rest. That meant that his father had finished building the hut.

When he saw that this father had finished building the hut, Nshnkati rolled the ball to the child of the Wind and exclaimed, "There it goes! O Izhrriten-kuan-kuan! There it goes! O Igau-Igaubu-ti! There it goes!" And he scampered away. He ran home as fast as he could.

The son of the Wind began to lean over, sputtering. He fell down. He lay kicking violently upon the ground.

The people's huts vanished. They blew away. The bushes shattered. The people could not see anything for the dust.

The child of the Wind's mother came out of her hut and picked her son up. She set him on his feet. Even so, he kicked and screamed and howled for a while. Then he grew tired and became still.

We who are Bushmen, we say, "The wind seems to be laying down, for it is kicking and blowing straight across the earth." But we do not like to mention the Wind's name or the names of his children. Otherwise we might call them up.

The Wind

The Wind was once a man. He became a bird. And he was flying. He no longer walked, as he used to do. He was flying. He made a home in the mountain, in a cave in the mountain. He was flying. He was formerly a man.

He became a bird, and he was flying, and he rested in a mountain cave. He was coming out of it, he flew about, and he returned to it. And he came to sleep in it; and, awaking early, he goes out of it; he flies away, again, he flies away. And he again returns, and he goes out, about, about, about, about, he again returns. This is how the Wind behaves, always moving around.

Kagara and Haunu,
Who Fought Each Other with Lightning

Kagara and Haunu were brothers-in-law. One day they argued over something. Kagara went to fetch his younger sister, to take her away from Haunu and take her back to her parents.

Haunu gave chase to his brother-in-law. He passed along behind the hill in pursuit of them.

The clouds came, clouds that were unequaled in beauty, and vanished away.

Kagara said to his sister, "You must walk on." His younger sister walked, carrying a heavy burden of her things and her husband's things. Kagara said, "You must walk on, for home is not near at hand."

Haunu passed along behind the hill.

The clouds came, the clouds vanished away.

Kagara said to his sister, "You must walk on, for you have keen sight and will be able to tell when we are nearing our parents' home." When she saw their house growing nearer, she told him so, and Kagara said, "Walk on! Walk on!" He waited for his younger sister. She came up to his side. He exclaimed, "What things can these be, so heavy that they make you walk so slowly?"

Then Haunu came upon them. He sneezed. Blood poured out of his nostrils as he rained lightning on his brother-in-law. His brother-in-law fended him off. His brother-in-law threw lightning right back at him. Haunu fended off his brother-in-law in return. Kagara said to his sister, "You must come and walk close beside me, for you the one who your husband is chasing. He is not giving us much time to escape. He is sending much lightning our way. You can see that he wants to harm us."

Kagara and Haunu went along, angry with each other. Haunu had intended to destroy Kagara with lightning. But Kagara was strong. He continued to fend off Haunu. His younger sister's husband threw countless bolts of lightning at him, and he threw countless bolts of lightning at his brother-in-law in reply.

Kagara finally threw black lightning, The lightening whisked Haunu up and carried him off.

Kagara's younger sister's husband, his brother-in-law, lay dying. He lay dying, slowly thundering. Haunu lay thundering; he thundered there, while Kagara went to lie down. He rubbed himself with wild rose and then he lay down and slept.

!khwǎ kǎ χóro ; or, water-bull.

An animal which is said to live in the water, and to be captured by the sorcerers and led about the country by them when they want to make rain.

Dǐä!kwǎiṅ, May , 1875.

A Woman of the Early Race and the Rain Bull

The Rain courted a young woman, while the young woman was in her hut. She felt ill and tired. The Rain scented her, and the place became misty. And she lay there, that young woman, smelling the Rain's scent, while the place was fragrant, while the place filled with the Rain's breath.

The young woman became aware of him. The Rain lowered his tail, which was the wispy tail of a cloud. The young woman exclaimed, "Who can this man be who comes to me in a cloud?"

The young woman took up wild rose in her hand. She threw it upon his forehead. And she arose, she pressed the wild rose down upon his forehead, she pushed him away, and she wrapped herself in her leather cloak.

She mounted the Rain, and the Rain took her away. She went along in the sky, looking at the trees far below. And as she went along, she said to the Rain, "You must go to that tree over there, the big one, and set me down beside it." The Rain trotted along, taking her straight to that large tree. He set her down close to the trunk. The young woman looked at him. She smiled, and took out wild rose, and rubbed him with it. The wild rose soothed the Rain, and he went to sleep.

When she saw that the Rain slept, she climbed up, she stole softly away, she climbed up, she climbed the tree. And she climbed down far from where the Rain lay sleeping. She softly returned home. The rain awoke behind her back, when the place where he slept had grown cool.

He arose. He walked away, shaking off sleep. He went away to the middle of the spring where he lived, believing that the young woman was still sitting on his back. He went away, he went away to the water. He went into it.

The young woman was at home all this time. She went to burn wild rose, because she smelled strongly of the scent of the tree. She rubbed herself with wild rose smoke to take off the smell of the tree.

The Rain was unaware. But the old women of the village, who had been out seeking food and saw all these things as they happened, came home and started to burn horns. They wanted to be sure that the smell of the horns would rise up around their huts, and not the smell of the tree or the wild rose, so that the Rain would not be angry with them.

Songs

The Cat's Song

Ha ha ha,
Ha ha,
I am the one whom the Lynx derides,
I am the one who did not run fast;
The Lynx is the one who runs fast.
Ha ha ha,
Ha ha.
I am the one whom the Lynx derides.
Ya ya ya,
Ya ya,
I am the one whom the Lynx derides.
I am the one who could not run fast.
Ya ya ya,
ya ya,
I am the one whom the Lynx derides,
"The Cat could not run fast."
Ya ya ya,
ya ya,
The Cat is the one whom the Lynx derides,
"It is the one who could not run fast,"
ya ya ya,
ya ya,
"The Cat is the one who could not run fast,
It was not cunning.
It did foolish things.
The Lynx is one who understands,

The Cat does not understand."
But the Cat is cunning.
Ya ya ya
Ya ya.
The Cat is the one about whom the Lynx talked.
"It is the one who could not run fast."
It had to be cunning.
For the Lynx is one who is cunning.
Haggla haggla haggla
Haggla haggla,
Heggle heggle heggle,
Heggli,
Heggli heggli heggli
Heggli n!

The Song of the Caama Fox

Crosser of the Spoor, Crosser of the Spoor,
Crosser of the Spoor, Crosser of the Spoor!

Cross the Caama Fox's spoor,
cross the Caama Fox's spoor!

Cross the Caama Fox's spoor,
cross the Caama Fox's spoor!

The Songs of the Blue Crane

1.
This is the Blue Crane's song. It is carrying krieboom berries on its shoulders as it goes along singing:

The berries are upon my shoulder,
The berries are upon my shoulder,
the berries are upon my shoulder.
The berries are upon my shoulder,
the berries are up here on my shoulder,
rrru are up here.
The berries are up here,
rrru are up here,
are up here.
The berries *rru* are put away upon my shoulder.

2. *(Sung when running away from a man)*

A splinter of white stone,
a splinter of white stone,
a splinter of stone that is white.

3. *(Sung when walking slowly, leaving a place)*

A white stone splinter,
a white stone splinter.

4. (Sung when it flaps its wings)

Scrape the springbok skin for a bed.
Scrape the springbok skin for a bed.
Rrrru rrra,
Rrru rrra,
Rru rra!

The Old Woman's Song

(First version)

The old woman sings; goes singing along; sings as she goes;
the old woman sings as she goes along about the hyena:

The old she-hyena,
the old she-hyena,
was carrying off the old woman from her hut.
The old woman sprang aside,
she arose,
she beat the hyena,
the hyena herself,
she killed the hyena.

(Second version)

The old she-hyena,
the old she-hyena,
was carrying off the old woman
as the old woman lay in her hut."

A Song Sung by the Star Gaunu, and by Bushman Women

Does the *garraken* flower open?
The *kugham* is the one that opens.
Do you open?
The *kugham* is the one that opens.

Sirius and Canopus

Sirius!
Sirius!
winks like
Canopus!

Canopus
winks like
Sirius!

Canopus
winks like
Sirius!

Sirius
winks like
Canopus!

The Song of the Bustard

My younger brother-in-law
put my head in the fire.
My younger brother-in-law,
my younger brother-in-law
put my head in the fire.

When we startle the bustard, it flies away; it cries *Wara
'khau, wara 'khau, wara 'khau, 'khau 'khau, 'khau, wara 'khau,
wara 'khau, 'khau, 'khau, 'khau, 'khau!"* When it stands on the
ground, it says: *"A wa, a wa, a wa, a wa!"* when it stands on the
ground.

The Song of the Springbok Mothers

The springbok mothers sang, soothing their children,

> *A-a hn,*
> O springbok child!
> Sleep for me.
> *A-a hn,*
> O springbok child!
> Sleep for me.

A Song on the Loss of a Tobacco Pouch

Famine it is,
Famine it is,
Famine is here.

Famine it is,
Famine it is,
Famine is here.

Famine: a Bushman could not smoke, because a dog had come in the night and carried off his tobacco pouch. He arose in the night, he missed his pouch. And then he again lay down, because he could not smoke. And we were seeking the pouch. We did not find the pouch.

The Broken String

There were people
who broke the string for me.
Therefore,
the place became like this to me,
silent,
on account of it,
because the string broke.
Therefore,
the place does not feel to me
as the place used to feel to me,
on account of it.
The place feels as if it stood open before me,
because the string has broken.
Therefore,
the place does not feel pleasant to me,
on account of it.

The Death of the Lizard

The Lizard formerly sang:

For,
I therefore intend to go,
passing through
the pass of Guru 'nah.

And,
I therefore intend to go,
passing through
the pass of Xe 'khwai.

For,
I therefore intend to go,
passing through
the pass of Guru 'nah.

And,
I therefore intend to go,
passing through
the pass of Xe 'khwai.

When the lizard was passing through, the mountains squeezed him and broke him. The mountains bit him and broke him. His front half fell over and stood still. It became the mountain called Guru 'nah. His rear half fell over and stood still. It became the mountain called Xe 'khwai.

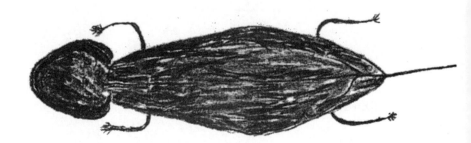

1.

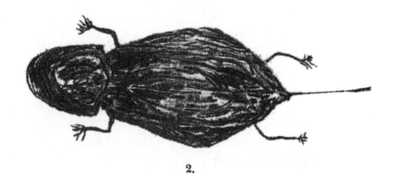

2.

Lizards of the Genus *Agama*.
1. *!khǫ́ú gwaī*, male. 2. *!khǫ́ú !aītyi*, female.

Díä!kwǎin, March, 1875

The Song of the Leopard

The leopard formerly sang:

> *Hn-n, hn;*
> I kill children who cry;
> *Hn-n, hn.*
> I kill children who cry;
> *Hn-n, hn.*
> I kill children who cry.

A beast of prey he is. My grandfather used to say that the leopard formerly said:

> *Hn-n, hn;*
> I kill children who cry;
> *Hn-n, hn.*
> I kill children who cry.

When my grandfather wanted us to stop making noise, he said that the leopard used to say:

> *Hn-n, hn;*
> I kill children who cry;
> *Hn-n, hn.*
> I kill children who cry.

And when the leopard hears a little child crying there, he follows the sound to it, while the little child is crying there, he, following the sound, goes to it, approaches it stealthily, approaching, stealthily, reaches the hut in which the little child is crying. He springs, springs into the hut. He catches hold of the little child, he springs, taking it away. He goes to swallow it down. He departs.

Prayer to the Young Moon

Young Moon!
Hail, Young Moon!
Hail, hail,
Young Moon!
Young Moon! speak to me!
Hail, hail,
Young Moon!
Tell me something.
Hail, hail!
When the sun rises,
you must speak to me,
so that I may eat something.
You must speak to me about a little thing,
so that I may eat.
Hail, hail,
Young Moon!

Hunters

The Leopard and the Jackal

The jackal watches the leopard when the leopard has killed a springbok. The jackal whines, begging for springbok flesh. He howls, he begs, for he is a jackal. Therefore he howls. When he begs, he may eat.

Then the leopard is angry, the leopard kills him, the leopard bites him dead, he lifts him up, he goes to put him into the bushes; thus he hides him.

Doings of the Springbok

The mother springbok does this as she trots along next to her kid. She grunts as she trots along, saying *"a, a, a"* as she trots along. The springbok make a resounding noise because they are so many; the springbok kids bleat while their mothers grunt. Their mothers say *"a, a, a,"* and the springbok kids say *"me, me, me"* while their mothers say *"a, a, a"* as they grunt. The springbok children say *"me, me, me, me,"* while their mothers say *"a, a, a"* as they grunting go forward.

The Bushmen say: "O beast of prey! You are the one who hears the place behind us. It is resonant with sound. Therefore, I said that I would sit here. For these male springbok that stand around, they are the ones that will go along, passing behind you; because I am lying down, and they do not see me, they will come along, passing behind you, when you have gone behind the hill; they will come along, passing behind you."

Habits of the Bat and the Porcupine

Mama said to me that the bat stays with the porcupine when it looks for food. When the porcupine returns home, then it is that the bat comes to its hole, which they share. Then I know that the porcupine has returned.

Mama told me about it, that I should watch for the porcupine if I saw the bat. I must not sleep; for I must watch for the porcupine; for, when the porcupine approaches, I feel sleepy, I become sleepy. For the porcupine makes us sleep against our will, so that we do not know when it comes home. It wants to come to its hole while we are asleep. Therefore, it goes along making us sleep. And it smells the air to see whether harm awaits it at the hole, whether a man is lying in wait for it at the hole. And if the man is asleep it steals softly away, lifting its quills so that they do not rattle.

Therefore mama used to tell me that even it I felt sleepy, I should know that the porcupine was the one who went along making me sleepy against my will; it was the one who went along causing me to sleep. I should do thus, even if I felt that I wanted to sleep, I should not sleep; for the porcupine would come, if I slept there. And the porcupine would steal gently away while I slept. I should not know the time at which the porcupine came; I should think that the porcupine had not come, while the porcupine had long come; it had come and gone away while I slept. Therefore, I should not sleep, so that I might know when the porcupine came.

Therefore, when I lie in wait for a porcupine, I do not sleep when I am watching for the porcupine. The porcupine comes while I am watching for it. I see it return, for I am the one who did not sleep. For mama was the one who told me that I must not sleep, even if I felt sleepy; I must do as my father used to do, when father watched for the porcupine. My father used to know when the porcupine came. Even if he felt sleepy, he did not sleep, because he wanted to know the time at which the porcupine came.

These things my mother and the others told me: namely, that the porcupine does not go about at noon; it goes about by night, for it cannot see at noon. Night is the time when it sees well.

Father used to tell me that the porcupine returns when the Milky Way turns back. Father taught me about the stars. He said that when lying in wait at a porcupine's hole, I should watch the stars, especially the place where the stars fall. The porcupine is really where the stars fall, searching for food there.

I must also feel the wind. The porcupine will not return coming right out of the wind. It returns crossing the wind in a slanting direction, because it wants to smell the air. Therefore, it goes across the wind in a slanting direction, because it wants to smell whether harm is at this place.

Father used to tell me that I must not breathe strongly when lying in wait for a porcupine, for it hears everything. I should also not rustle strongly, for a porcupine hears everything. Therefore, we turn ourselves gently when we sit, so that the porcupine does not hear us.

!χ̣ó̱ gwāi, male porcupine.

｜hȧṅ‡kass'ŏ, Jan. 26th, 1879

!x̣ó⊙p̣u̱á, young porcupine.　‡nèrru, birds.

｜hȧṅ‡kass'ŏ, Mowbray, June 26th, 1879

｜kúkẹn-tĕ̆ ｜āiti, female anteater.

｜hȧṅ‡kass'ŏ, Oct., 1878

!xó⊙pụá, young porcupine. ǂnèrru, birds.

lhdñǂkass'ō, Mowbray, June 26th, 1879

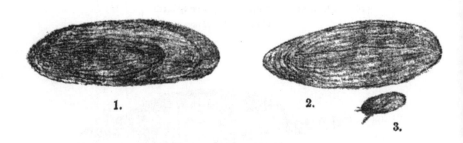

1.   2.   3.

Mountains into which the ǀkhdù (a lizard of the Genus *Agama*)
was changed when cut into two pieces.

1. ǀguru-lnā.   2. ǀχé ǀkhwái.   3. ǀχé ǀkhwái ta ǀkàù ka tï-⊙pụá.

lhañǂkass'ō, 1878

The Kaukau Bird and the Wild Cat

The kaukau bird says *"Tcha, tcha, tcha, tcha"* when it laughs at the wild cat. It has seen the cat. The cat is lying down, lying asleep, and it is laughing at the cat on account of it.

The other little birds, hearing it, flock to the kaukau bird. They are all laughing at the cat.

The Baboons and the Hunter

The baboons spied a Bushman hunter as he was coming away from the white men whom he had been to visit. He was carrying a sack of flour, which the white men gave him. The baboons said, "Uncle Hunter is returning home. Let's cross his path and knock him down."

The baboons scampered up to the hunter. The hunter asked them what they were up to. The hunter remarked on how steep their foreheads were. "Hey, beetlebrows, run away!" he cried. "Your heads look like rock ledges!"

The baboons angrily came up to the hunter, carrying sticks, meaning to beat him. The baboons' children also came. They called out to their parents, "O fathers! You must give us that man's head, so that we can play with it."

The hunter heard all this and thought to himself, "What shall I do? There are so many of those baboons." He thought, "I'll climb a krieboom and sit above them. If the baboons want me, they'll have to drag me down from the krieboom."

He climbed the krieboom. The baboons went up to him, as he sat above them in the krieboom. The baboon's children spoke to each other, saying, "Have a look at that man's big head. It will keep us entertained for a long time when we get the chance to play with it. See how big it is! It won't break anytime soon."

A grownup baboon spoke to the children, saying, "Why do you think you'll get to have some of that man? He belongs to us! We grownups will keep his pieces."

And the hunter thought to himself, "How am I going to get those baboons to leave me alone? They're angry now." He thought to himself, "I'll have to tell the white men about these baboons. Baboons are afraid of guns, after all."

He thought about this for a little longer, then he called out loudly, saying, "O white men! Come and help me. These baboons are bothering me. You must come and shoot them and drive them away from me."

The baboons looked around. They didn't see any white men, but they thought they had better not take any chances. The baboons ran away. The hunter quickly descended from the krieboom. He ran away in the other direction, escaping from the baboons, who ran all the way to those cliffs over there.

A Lion's Story

A child once cried for ant eggs. Hearing her, a lion came. Her parents lay asleep, and she sat by them, crying.

The lion thought, "Hmmm. I can eat the child. Or I can eat the parents. Maybe I'll eat them all."

While the lion sat there and pondered, the child pulled a brand out of the fire, and she pulled out some dry grass from under her mother, who was using it as a mattress. Her mother stirred a little but did not wake up. The child took the grass and set it on fire. She threw the grass out into the bush, and the bushes caught on fire. The flames swallowed that lion up, and the lion died.

And the child's mother gave her plenty of ant eggs afterward, and pieces of cooked ostrich egg, for she saw the dead lion and knew that her child had been the one to set it on fire.

The Man Who Found a Lion in a Cave

My grandfather once told me that a man long ago did thus. Once when he was out walking a heavy, drenching rain began to fall, and so he thought that he would go and sleep in a cave. But really a lion had been the one who had made the rain in order to confuse the man, so that he would not know where his home was, so that he might pass by his home in the darkness and go to a different place where the lion could get hold of him and eat him.

The place was very dark, and he stumbled about in the bush, for he could not see the path along which he was walking. He thought, "I must look for a cave to sleep in, if I can find one. I can return home in the morning. It's raining too hard to go on."

There was a cave not far away. The lion had come first to the cave. It came to lie in wait for the man.

The lion was wet, too. When it had sat for a little while inside the cave, it became warm, and, comfortable, it slept, thinking that it would hear the man when he came inside the cave. Then, the lion thought, it would catch hold of the man.

So the lion had thought. But it fell fast asleep all the same.

The man came into the cave. He heard something breathe. The man thought, "Can people have come to the cave? Is that who is breathing here?"

And then he thought, "How is that these people do not talk, if indeed they are really people? Can the people have fallen fast asleep? Why don't they speak to me?"

And then he thought, "I will not call out to these people, for I do not know whether they really are people. First I will feel gently about with my hands. That way I can tell whether they are really people. That would be better than calling out to wake them up."

He felt about. He felt that a thing that seemed to have hair. He poked around a little, and then he decided that what he was feeling was a lion's paw.

The man gently stepped backward and turned round. He went out of the cave on tiptoe.

When he had gone to a little distance, he ran swiftly, because he thought that the lion would smell his scent and run to catch him.

And when he had gone to a little distance, when a little time had passed, he heard the lion. The lion had smelled his scent and awakened, growling, and had clawed out at the air where the man had been standing only a few minutes earlier.

The man heard the lion's roar, and the man exclaimed, "It sounds as if the lion has caught my scent!"

And the man thought that he had better not go home, but instead run to a different place. He knew that the lion would find his tracks and catch up to him. He would hide in a different place and then, at daybreak, he would make his way home, when he could see the path – if, that is, the lion had not killed him in the meanwhile.

When the sun's rays began to make the sky pink at dawn, the man was still running. He had heard the lion running along behind him all night long, chasing him.

As he ran along, he saw the fire of some Bushmen. He thought that the people were probably standing around it, warming themselves. And he thought, "I will run to the fire over there and sleep among the people. Perhaps they will keep me safe from the lion."

And he thought, "Wait a minute. The lion's eye sometimes resembles a fire by night. I had better make sure that it is a real fire that burns there."

And he ran nearer to the fire. He looked, and he saw that people were lying around in front of the fire, warm and secure. And he thought, "I will go to these people, for it seems as if they really are people."

And he went to the people. And he told the people about what had happened to him. "Do you think that I have not walked into death this night? It just happened that the lion slept. That is why you see me now! You would not have seen me had the lion not slept. But it slept, and so I am able come to you for help."

He told the other people about it. They did not believe him at first, for who can escape a lion? But then the lion came by, saying, "Where is the man who came to my cave? I smell its tracks nearby!"

Day broke while the lion was still threatening them. When the day broke, the lion went away, leaving the people. Otherwise it would have caught and killed that man. For the lion does not come to us when the sun stands in the sky.

4.

9.

5.

8.

7.

6.

1.

2.

3.

Row of sticks with feathers tied upon them, used in springbok-hunting, to turn the game. The lines represent the Bushmen lying in wait for them.

1. From this direction the herd of springbok comes.
2. Here they go towards the row of sticks with feathers tied upon them.
3. Here stands a woman, who throws up dust into the air.
4. This man, whose sticks they are, lies at their head.

Ihani‡kass'ō, Dec., 1878

Some Hunting Observations

When we want to show respect to the game we chase, we act in this manner, so that the game sees that we respect it and will die willingly to help us live. For the game will not die if we did not show it respect.

We do as follows: first, we make sure to eat animals that have not run fast. For we desire the game to behave as the animals we have caught. If we killed a fast-running animal, then all the animals would run fast, and we would not eat. The game acts like the flesh we have eaten. Therefore, the old people give us the flesh of an animal that is not fleet.

When we have shot a gemsbok, the old people do not give us springbok flesh. For the springbok travels far, even at night; when day breaks, it is still walking about. Therefore the old people do not give us springbok meat. They believe that the game, if we ate springbok meat, would do as the springbok does. It would run far away, for the springbok does not sleep, even if it is night. The game would also do what the springbok does, going without sleep, wandering far away, traveling deep into the night.

The old people also do not allow us to take hold of the springbok's meat with our hands, because our hands, with which we hold our bows and arrows, should not take hold of the thing's flesh. We shot the thing, but if we held the meat our hands would not be able to catch its scent, and we would fail in the hunt. If we take hold of springbok meat, our hands will fail us. We think, "How can that be? I have smelled springbok meat before. How can I not shoot a springbok? Why are my hands failing me?" And some clever man will say, "You must have taken hold of springbok flesh, and so your hands cannot smell the springbok."

The man who shot the springbok is not allowed to carry the body. The old people let him sit down at a little distance, not near the place where the people are cutting up the springbok. He sits at a little distance, because he fears that he might smell the springbok's guts. That is why he sits at a little distance, because he does not want to smell the springbok's guts, which would keep him from smelling a springbok out on the veldt.

The Bushmen also put an animal's bones nicely aside. They do not throw them about. They put down the bones opposite to the entrance to a hut. They call this spot "the heap of meat bones."

The person who lives in that hut gnaws the bones, putting them on an ostrich breastbone. When he has finished gnawing the bones, he takes up the bones, and he puts them down at this place.

And when the other people have boiled other bones, they again gnaw at them, putting them on the ostrich breastbone dish when they are done eating. When they have finished gnawing the bones, they take up the ostrich breastbone and put it opposite the entrance to the other man's hut. The other man takes the bones he has gnawed, and he puts them opposite someone else's hut. Another man also does this, when he has gnawed the bones, he also puts the bones opposite the entrance of someone else's hut. That way everyone has a heap of bones.

They also do this when they cut up a springbok: they take out the stomach, and they shake out the contents of the stomach opposite to the entrance of the other one's hut. They shake out the contents of the stomach there on the other one's heap of bones. They pour blood into the stomach and dip up

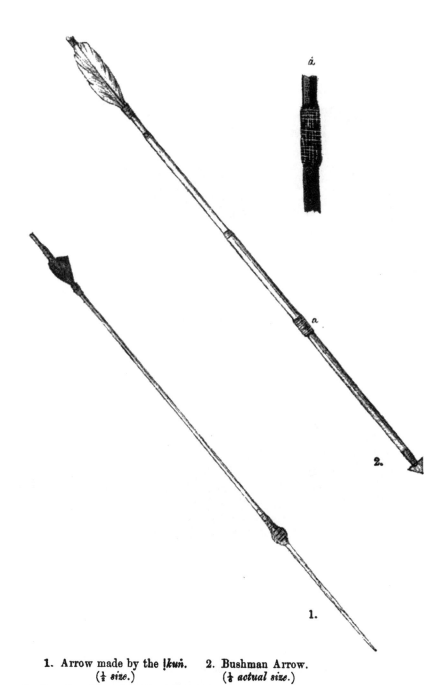

1. Arrow made by the !kuṅ.   2. Bushman Arrow.
   (½ size.)   (⅕ actual size.)
a. Section showing red marks by which the arrows are recognised
by Bushmen.

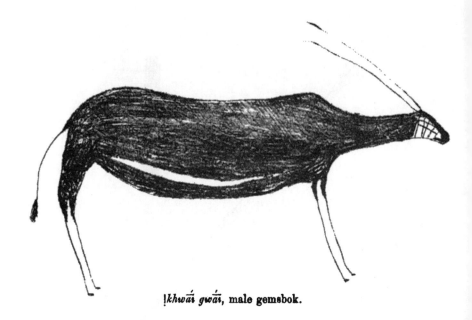

!khwā́ı gwā́ı, male gemsbok.

!khwā́ı lā́ıtyr̄, female gemsbok.

Diä!kwī̆in, April, 1875.

the blood with their hand, making a shape like a tortoiseshell with their hand. If any blood has spilled, they gather it up with the earth on which it lies, together with the bushes on which there is blood. Then they put them down opposite to the entrance of the other man's hut.

With regard to the *kaoken* bones, the bones that the children break to eat marrow, they also collect them and put them down opposite to the entrance of the other one's hut.

With regard to the shoulder blade bones, when they have gnawed at them, they put them away in their own huts, because they do not want the dogs to crunch them. If the dogs got hold of the bones, the man who shot the springbok would miss his aim.

They take the bones of the upper foreleg to the man who shot the springbok, so that his child can eat the marrow from them. They keep the shoulder blade bones to gnaw on later, in their huts.

They cut off the back of the springbok's neck, and they take it to the man who killed the springbok. They boil the springbok's back. They gnaw its bones, together with the tail. Their wives make soft bags from the leather, which the Bushmen use to carry things that they catch or get in barter. The people give their bags to the man who has killed the springbok, and in exchange he gives them things such as arrows and poison for the arrows.

Dreams and Beliefs

Bushman Presentiments

The Bushmen's knowledge lies deep within their bodies. The letters deep inside them speak. They move. They make the Bushmen's bodies move.

The Bushmen order the others to be silent when they feel the letters moving. A man stands altogether still when he feels that his body is tapping inside. A dream speaks falsely. It is a thing that deceives. A premonition speaks the truth. It tells a Bushman when there is meat about when it has tapped. The Bushmen perceive people coming by means of it. The Bushmen feel a tapping when other people are coming.

With regard to an old wound, a Bushman feels a tapping at the wound's place, whether it is his wound or someone else's. The one man feels the other man who comes. He says to the children, "Look around, for grandfather seems to be coming. This is why I feel the place of his body's old wound." The children look around. The children see the man coming. They say to their father, "A man is coming yonder." Their father says to them: "Grandfather comes yonder. I felt him at the place of his old wound. I wanted you to see that he is really coming. My presentiment speaks truly."

He feels a tapping at his ribs, and he says to the children, "The springbok seem to be coming, for I feel the black hair on the sides of the springbok. Climb atop the hill and look around at all the places. For I feel the springbok sensation."

The other man agrees with him. "I think that the children should do so," he says, "for the springbok come in the sun, and the hill is high. They children can look down and see the whole ground. They can look inside the trees, where the springbok like to go and hide. They can look into the little riverbeds where the springbok eat. The little riverbeds have become green. I feel a sensation in the calves of my legs when the springbok's blood is going to run down them. I always feel blood, when I am about to kill springbok. I now sit feeling a sensation behind my back, where the blood runs down when I am carrying a springbok. The springbok hair lies behind my back."

The other agrees with him, saying, "Yes, my brother."

Therefore, we wait quietly when the sensation is like this, when we are feeling the things come, while the things come near the house. We have a sensation in our feet, as we feel the rustling of springbok's feet, making the bushes rustle. We feel in this manner, we have a sensation in our heads when we are about to chop the springbok's horns. We have a sensation in our face on account of the blackness of the stripe on the face of the springbok. We feel a sensation in our eyes on account of the black marks on the eyes of the springbok. We feel the sensation of a louse when an ostrich is out walking, scratching the louse, when it is spring, when the sun feels warm.

Then it is that the things go from us. They go along, passing opposite our huts. We cross the animals' spoor when we go to hunt. Many things come along when we are lying in the shade of the hut, because they think that we are probably lying asleep in the noonday heat. This is true, for we really do lie down to nap in the noonday heat. But we do not lie sleeping at noon when we feel this sensation. For we feel like this when the things are walking, when we have felt the things coming, as they walk, moving their legs. We feel a sensation in the hollows under our knees, on which blood drops as we go along carrying the game. We feel this sensation there.

Therefore, the little boys do not lie in the shade inside the hut. They lie in the shade of the trees on the hill above, so that they can signal to us when they see game moving. They will beckon, making us see. We say to each other that the children appear to have seen things, for they beckon.

They point to the place where the animals are walking, our where the mountains lie spread out. They signal us so that we may quickly chase the game. The things walk, putting themselves in front of the hill; we will quickly pass behind it, away from the springbok. We will stand ready for the game. We will steal up on the game, confronting their leader at the place where he goes.

Prayers for the Arrival of Canopus and Sirius

The Bushmen see Canopus, and they say to a child, "Give me a piece of wood, so that I can put the end of it in the fire, so that I may point it toward grandmother. Grandmother carries ant eggs, and she is cold. The sun will warm grandmother's eye for us so that she can see where the ant eggs are hiding."

Sirius comes out, and the people call out to one another, saying, "Sirius comes yonder."

They say to one another, "You must burn a stick for us, pointing it in the direction of Sirius."

They say to one another, "Who was it who saw Sirius?"

One man says to the other, "Our brother saw Sirius."

The other man says to him, "I saw Sirius."

The other man says to him, "Burn a stick for us, pointing it toward Sirius, so that the sun will come out for us, so that Sirius will not stay in the sky forever and make us cold."

The other man, the one who saw Sirius, says to his son, "Bring me the small piece of wood over there so that I can put the end of it in the fire, pointing it toward grandmother, so that grandmother can ascend high into the sky, like the other one, Canopus."

The child brings him the piece of wood. The father holds the end of it in the fire. He points it burning toward Sirius. He says that Sirius shall twinkle like Canopus. He sings about Canopus, he sings about Sirius. He points to them with fire, so that they may twinkle like each other. He throws fire at them.

He covers himself up entirely, from his head to his toes, in his cloak, and he lies down.

He arises. He sits down. But he does not lie down, because he feels that he has more work to do to putting the sun's warmth into Sirius, so that Sirius may be warm.

The women go out early to seek ant eggs. They walk, sunning their shoulder blades.

The Use of the *Goin-goin*

The people beat the *goin-goin* drum so that the bees may become abundant, so that the bees may go into their places, so that the people may eat honey. The people beat the *goin-goin* so that they may cut and gather honey, that they may put honey away into bags.

And the people carry honey the honey home. And the people take honey to the women at home. For the women are dying of hunger at home. The men take honey to the women at home, and the women, no longer hungry, make drums for them so that they may dance – for they do not frolic when they are hungry.

And they dance, those men, when the women have made drums for them. The men dance while the women sit down, clapping their hands for the men. One women beats the drum, while the others clap their hands for the men as they are dancing.

The sun rises while they are dancing there, satisfied with the food they have eaten. The sun rises while they are dancing there, while the women are satisfied with the food. The sun shines on the backs of their hands, which are covered with the dust of the drums. The men are covered with dust, while the dust of the drums coats the women's faces, the dust that the men's feet have made as they dance strongly on the earth. The dust rises up from their feet, it rises up among them, as they stand dancing. They dance.

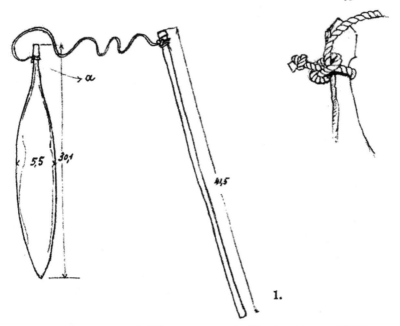

Length of string in **Fig. 1** = 48 cm., in **Fig. 2** = 54 cm.   Thickness
of wood about 3–4 mm.   The edges are sharpened.

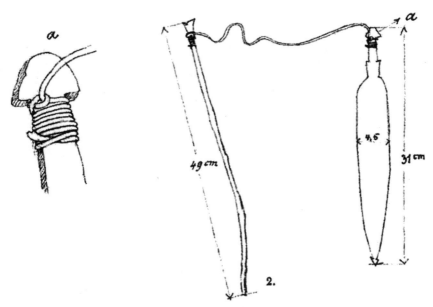

Instruments similar to *!göȧn-!göȧn*, made by the *!kuȧ*.

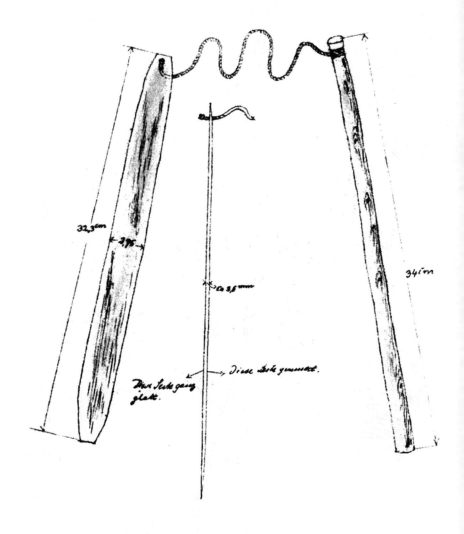

Length of the (once-twisted) string = 40·5 cm.
!GÓÏN-!GÓÏN.

Then they sleep, letting the sun set. They are tired when they have been dancing there, after the women leave off drumming. The place becomes dark, as they sleep there, because they are tired, when they have danced there.

Morning is the time when they send the children to the water, so that the children may dip up water for them, so that they may drink, for they are very thirsty. The children go early to dip up water for them, at the break of day, so that they may come to drink. For they are thirsty. They are not aware that they are tired. They send the children to the water, for they are thirsty.

Getting Rid of Bad Dreams

My mother used to do this, when she intended to go out to seek food. When she was about to start, she took a stone and plunged the stone into the ashes of the fire. As she did, she exclaimed, "I am going yonder. You stay!" She wished that the evil things about which she had been dreaming should remain in the fire, instead of going out with her. If she did not act in this way, she said, they would go out with her. The place to which she went would not be nice, because she had dreamed of evil things that were not nice. She acted in this manner because she knew that if she went out with the dream, she would have bad luck.

The ant eggs would avoid her, because they would know that she had dreamed evil things. The ant eggs would be aware that mama had dreamed evil things, and they would stay far away from her.

Two Apparitions

We buried my wife in the afternoon. When we had finished burying her, we returned to the home of my sister and her people. They had come to bury my wife with me. When we had buried my wife, we went away, crossing over the salt pan.

And we saw a thing that looked like a little child. It sat on the salt pan, with its legs crossed over each other.

My sister spoke, she questioned us, "Look! What is that thing sitting over there on the salt pan? It looks like a little child."

And another sister spoke, she asked us, "Look! Why is it that this thing seems like a person? It looks as if it has on the cap that our brother's wife used to wear."

And my sister spoke, she answered, "Yes, O my younger sister! The cap looks like the one our brother's wife wore." The apparition seemed as if it sat looking toward the place from which we had come.

And the younger sister spoke, she said, "The old people used to tell me that the angry people acted thus: at the time when they took a person away, they used to allow the person to appear in front of us in some form, so that we might see that person one last time. You know our brother's wife had a very little child. You should allow us to look at the thing that sits on the salt pan. It resembles a person, someone we know."

And I spoke. I said, "Wait! Let us return home and see if we see it again."

We went to my sister's home. We talked there for a little while. Then I said that although they probably that I did not wish to return home, because the sun was setting, I was going to go. I thought that I go by way of the path on which we had come, so that I could see whether I would see the apparition again, sitting out there on the salt pan. Going along, I looked at the place where it had sat. I thought that it might have been a bush. I did not see it at the place where it had been sitting. And I agreed that it must have been a different kind of thing.

For our mothers used to tell us that when the sorcerers take us away, that is the time when our friend is in front of us, because he wants us to see him, because he wants us to know that he is still thinking of us. Therefore, his outer skin still looks at us, because he does not want to go away and leave us. He insists on coming to us one last time, and we see him.

My sister's husband told us that when he was hunting one day, as he was going along, he saw a little child peeping at him by the side of a bush. And he thought, "Can this be my child who has run after me? It seems to have lost its way. It seems to have followed me." And he thought: "Let me walk nearer, so that I may look at this child to see who it is."

And he saw that the child seemed to fear him. The child sat behind the bush. The child looked from side to side, acting as if it wanted to run away. And my sister's husband walked, going near it. The child arose and walked away, looking from side to side, acting as if it wanted to run away.

And he looked to see why the child did not wish him to come to it. The child seemed to be afraid of him. And he looked at the child as the child stood looking at him. He saw that it was a little girl. He saw that the child was like a person. He decided to let the child alone. And he walked on, while the child stood looking from side to side. And when the child saw that he was going away from it, it came forward near the bush and sat down again.

The Jackal's Heart Is Not to Be Eaten

The Bushmen feel that a little child is likely to be timid. Therefore, the little child does not eat jackals' hearts, because the jackal is very afraid. The jackal runs away whenever we approach it.

The leopard is the one whose heart the little child eats. The leopard is not afraid. A little child becomes a coward from eating the jackal's heart. If it eats the jackal's heart, its own heart fills with fear.

Therefore, we do not give the jackal's heart to a little child. We feel that the jackal is the kind of creature that runs away, even when it has not seen us, when it has only heard our feet rustle. It runs away, not even looking to see what the noise is.

Signs Made by Bushmen to Show
Where They Have Gone

The Bushmen are accustomed to do this: when another man has gone away and does not return, they push their feet along the ground, if they move from the place where they have been resting, and they place grass near the marks they have made. When the other man returns, he sees that they have gone away from their camp. He looks around, and he sees the grass standing upright.

And he exclaims, "The people must have traveled away to the water pool over there." And he goes to the water, looking for the people, to see whether the people have gone to spend time at that pool.

And, he goes, ascending the hill. He sits upon it, looking for our huts. And he sees the huts. He sits, looking at them, as the smoke of the fire rises from the huts. And he exclaims, "The people must be there!" And he arises, he goes to the huts, and he arrives safely at home.

And the other people, seeing the man's shape far away on the hill, exclaim, "Our brother must be the one who comes, for he knows the water and has followed our signs."

We also reverse branches. We place them so that their green top is underneath and the dry stump of the branch is uppermost. We draw our feet along the ground to make a mark. When the other man returns and sees that we are not there, he finds the branch and exclaims, "The people must have traveled away to that little pool. This is why they have reversed a branch, pointing in the direction of the place where the water is. I will go down to the water and look for the people's footprints." And he goes down to the water. And he goes to look at the water, and he sees the people's footprints, and he follows their path along to their camp.

A Bushman, Becoming Faint from the Sun's Heat, Throws Earth into the Air

A Bushman does this if he is returning home, if he feels as if he cannot reach his home because he is faint from the heat of the sun: he throws up earth into the air, because he wants the people at home to see the dust and come help him.

And the person who is looking out, sitting in the bushes to avoid the sun's heat, because it is very hot, she stands up and looks around. And as she stands looking around, she sees the dust, and she exclaims, "A person seems to be throwing up earth there!"

And the people run, run out of the house, exclaiming, "He throws up earth to let us know that he needs help! You must run quickly and give him water. For the sun is killing him. It is his heart. You must run to give him water."

The people run to the man. They go and find him, pouring water to cool the man.

And he first sits up to remove the darkness from his face, for the sun's darkness resembles night.

These are not women's doings. These are men's doings.

The Bushmen feel that as they chase things, as they chase the springbok, they become tired from running. The sun is killing them when they are tired. They go staggering along from fatigue. The fatigue goes out a little, and they become cool. Then they go staggering along, sweating to cool themselves, they go along staggering, and they feel as if they will never see their home again. This is when they sit down and throw up earth into the air. They throw up earth for the people at home, because they wish the people at home to see the dust and rescue them.

Death

The star does this at the time when our heart falls down: that is the time when the star also falls down, for the star feels that our heart has fallen over. The star falls down, too, for the stars know the time at which we die. The stars tell the other people who do not know that we have died.

Therefore, the people do this when they have seen a star that has fallen down. They say, "Look! Why is it that the star has fallen down? We shall hear news, for a star has fallen down. Some bad thing has happened somewhere. The star tells us that a bad thing has happened at another place."

The woodpecker acts in this manner when a star has fallen. It comes, and it flies over us, and it cries. The people say, "Did you not hear the woodpecker when the star fell? It came to tell us that our person is dead."

The people speak. They say that the woodpecker is not a thing that deceives, for it would not come to our home if it did not know that something bad had happened. When it knows that something bad has happened, then it comes to our home, because it wants to come and tell us about it, namely, that our person has died.

Therefore, our mothers and the other old people used to say, if they heard a woodpecker flying overhead, "Go and have a bath, for I know that you came to tell me something." They meant that the woodpecker should take this bad news to the Orange River's water, to the place where the stars stand in the water. That is the place where its stories should go in. For our mothers and the other old people did not want to hear the story that it came to tell. They knew that the woodpecker does this at the time a man dies. That is the time when it comes to us, when it tells us about it, tells us that the man has died. For, our mothers and the other old people used to say, the woodpecker lives beside that water in which we see all kinds of things before they happen. It knows what has happened before we do. It lives at the pool in which we see all things; the things that are in the sky we see in the water as we stand by the water's edge.

We see all things. The stars look like burning fires.

When it is night, when another man walks along the river, we see him as he walks, passing the water. It seems as if it were noonday, when he walks by the water. We see him clearly. The place seems as if it were midday as we see him walking along. Therefore, our mothers and the other old people said, when the woodpecker has seen in the water a person who has died, even though it be at a great distance, it knows that he is our relative and it flies away from the water, it flies to us, because it wants to tell us that our relative has died.

The woodpecker and the star are those who tell us about it when we have not heard the news. They are the ones who tell us about it, and when we have heard the woodpecker we also see the star, and then we know that someone close to us has died.

Our mothers and the other old people used to tell us that the Rain carries off young girls, and the girls remain at that water to which the Rain had taken them. They are girls with whom the Rain is angry. The Rain makes lightning, killing them. They become stars, those girls, and they no longer look like girls. They become stars. For, our mothers and the other people used to tell us, when the Rain has carried her off, a girl becomes like a flower that grows in the water.

If we did not know this, we would go to the water and see the flowers standing there, and we would see that they are so beautiful and think, "I will go and pick the flowers that are standing in the water, for they are very beautiful." Our mothers and the other old people said to us that the flowers, if they saw that we were coming toward them, would disappear in the water. Then we would think, "The flowers that were standing here, where are they? Why is it that I do not see them?" They would disappear in the water, and we would not see them again.

Therefore, our mothers and the other old people said, we should not go near the flowers that we see standing in the water, even if we see their beauty. For they are girls whom the Rain has taken away. They resemble flowers. They are the water's wives, and we look at them, leaving them alone, because that is how we would want others to treat us if we were also flowers.

Therefore, our mothers and the other old people do this: they do not let the Bushmen women walk about when the Rain comes, for they are afraid that the Rain intends to kill them with lightning. For the Rain does this: when it comes, it smells our scent, and it makes lightning. It makes lightning, killing us. Therefore, our mothers and the other old people told us, when the Rain falls on us and we walk passing through the Rain, if we see that the Rain is lightning in the sky we must quickly look toward the place where the lightning is coming from. The Rain tries to kill us by stealth. But if its thunderbolts have come near us, if we look toward the place where the lightning has come from, then we make the thunderbolts turn away from us. Our eye also shines like the Rain's thunderbolts. Therefore, the Rain appears to fear our eye. If we look toward it, toward the place of the lightning, then the Rain will pass over us. It respects our eye, which shines on it. Therefore, it goes over us. It goes to sit on the ground over there. It does not kill us.

Snakes, Lizards, and a Certain Small Antelope, When Seen Near Graves, Are to Be Respected

A snake that is near a grave, that snake we do not kill. For it is another person's snake, our dead person's snake, the dead person's snake. We do not kill it. We respect it. And if over a course of many days we see it often, we do not kill it. When we see it, we let it alone.

Another day, if we see a lizard, we follow the lizard's spoor. If the lizard has gone to the grave of a person, we respect the lizard. We do not kill the lizard. We let the lizard alone.

When we see an antelope, an antelope that is near our other person's resting place, that place where our other person has died, we respect the antelope. For the antelope is not a mere antelope. Its legs seem small, but the antelope is really the person who just died. It is a spirit antelope.

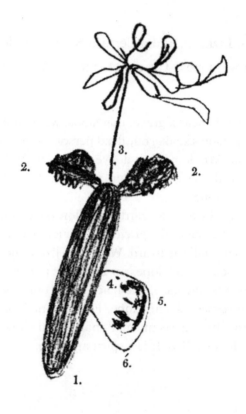

1 { **!kórro** / grave.   2 { **Ɣá.** / earth.   3 { **!kaṅ.** / tree.   *zău-ŭ* (the name of the tree, the berries and gum of which are eaten).

5 { **‖ke.** / the dead person.

4 { **!nụé.** / bag (the dead man's bag which is placed underneath his head).

6 { **‖gábbe.** / the little chamber or hole at the side of the grave, where the body is placed.

!nanni. *July 30th,* 1880

The Relations of Wind, Moon, and Cloud
to Human Beings after Death

The wind does thus when we die. Our own wind blows, for we, who are human beings, we possess wind, too. We make clouds when we die. When we die, the wind makes dust, because it intends to blow every trace of us away, taking away our footprints, the tracks we left on the ground as we walked about while there was nothing the matter with us. If the wind did not blow away our footprints, then we would see the tracks of everyone who had ever lived. It would be as if we were all still alive. Therefore, the wind blows, taking away our footprints.

Our gall, when we die, sits in the sky. It sits green in the sky when we are dead.

Therefore, our mothers would say this when the moon went to lie down, when the moon stood hollow: "The moon is carrying people who are dead. It lies on its side, it lies hollow, because it is starved from its exertions, starved from having to carry all the dead people. This is why it lies hollow. It is a bad moon, and you should expect to hear bad news when the moon is like this."

Those things in the sky that resemble clouds, we think they are clouds. We who do not know, we think they are clouds.

As for those of us who know, when we see clouds, we know that they are people. We sit looking at the clouds, as the clouds billow and make forms in the sky.

The hair of our heads will resemble clouds when we die.

III.—23. B.

THE GIRL OF THE EARLY RACE, WHO MADE STARS.*

(2505) Ṅ χ̇ŏ́ä ă ǂkákkă kĕ, tĭ ē, !kuíǁá kkóāṅ ǀhiṅ; hăṅ !kĭ ǀēyă hă ǀᵕkăǀᵕkă au !kúĭ; hăṅ ǁkāū kĭ ǁkāītẹn ǀkúĭ au !gwą́χ̇ŭ. Hăṅ ǂkákkă !kúĭ: "!kúĭ é ą́, hĭ
(2506) kkwą̆́ṅ ssĕ ǁkóä-kẹn ddí !kō. ( ) Hĭ ssĭṅ kkwą̆́ṅ ǀnĕ !kúĭtẹn !ā ttā !gwą́χ̇ŭ, ǀkụạǀkụáttẹn ssĕ !khé !uhí ttĭṅ !kō, au !kōwakẹn ǀnĕ ĕ !kō, au hĭ ssĭṅ ĕ !kúĭ." Hĭṅ ǁkóäkẹn ddī !kō. !kō ssĭṅ ǀnĕ ǁnwą̄rritẹn hĭ ǀkụạ-
(2507) ǀkụáttẹn; au !kōgẹn ( ) táttĭ ē, !kō ttēṅ ǁnwą́rritẹn; au ǀkuạǀkuáttẹn !gwéë-tẹn ǁā; hé tĭ hĭṅ ē, !kō ttēṅ-ă ǁā hĭ ǀkụạǀkụáttẹn. !kōgẹn ǁnaū tĭ ē, !kó kkăṅ !khē
(2508) !k'āū, ĭ; !kōgẹn ǁkụạṅ ǁnwą́rritẹn ( ) !ŭhā, au !kōgẹn kă, !kō ssĕ ǁkhaū !khéǃkhé, au !kógẹn táttĭ ē, ǀkụạ-ǀkụáttẹn ǀnĕ kkăṅ !χ̇uonnĭ; au ǀkụạǀkụáttakẹn tátti,
(2509) ǁkōĭṅ ā !χ̇uōńnĭyă; hăṅ ǀnĕ ( ) !uhí ssĭṅ hă-hă kă !χ̇árră; ǀkụạǀkụáttakẹn ǀnĕ !χ̇uōńni; au hĭṅ ǀnĕ ǂkam̆mă !gaúë; hĭ ssĕ-g ǀnĕ ttēn ákkẹn, au !kó wă-g ǀnĕ ttēn ákkẹn. ǀkụạǀkụáttẹn ssĕ-g ǀnĕ ǁχ̇ạḿ !khé

A page from *Specimens of Bushman Folklore* showing the transcription of the Bushman language

The Rock Rabbit and The Rainbow
Laurens van der Post among Friends

Edited by Robert Hinshaw

Sir Laurens van der Post loved the stories of the Bushman and was instrumental in making them known throughout the world. South African by birth, his extraordinary curiosity, his love for the small and the great, and his tremendous feeling and concern for his surroundings and all that they included, set him traveling the lands and the waters of the world, a messenger in search of meaning. He touched and inspired many along the way, some of whom are to be found in the pages of this book.

The Rock Rabbit and The Rainbow was originally conceived as a gift collection of writings for Sir Laurens by several of his friends and then evolved into its present form, which includes numerous original contributions by Sir Laurens himself.

400 pages, illustrated, hardcover, ISBN 3-85630-512-2

Alan McGlashan
The Savage and Beautiful Country

Alan McGlashan presents a sensitive view of the modern world and of time, of our memories and forgetfulness, joys and sorrows. He takes the reader on a safari into regions that are strange and yet familiar – into the savage and beautiful country of the mind. No "cures" are offered, but we are provoked to reflect on our roles and attitudes in the contemporary world jungle.

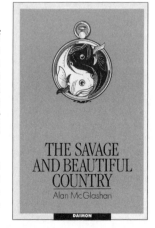

Alan McGlashan conveys a poetic vision which has more to do with life as it can be lived than all the experiments of the laboratory psychologist or the dialectic of the professional philosopher.
– The Times Literary Supplement

A highly provocative work, filled with astonishing and exciting insights about the less rational aspects of man, but communicated to the intelligent layman in an engagingly informal manner. – Library Journal

228 pages, ISBN 3-85630-517-3

A Testament to the Wilderness
Ten Essays on an Address by C. A. Meier
Edited by Robert Hinshaw

With their remarkably varied backgrounds yet common concerns for the physical and psychological environment, these prominent contributors – representing five continents – provide a gripping portrait of the wilderness today, both within and without.

This anthology of original writings was conceived in honor of the lifelong work of Prof. C.A. Meier of Zürich, on his eightieth birthday. It is recommended reading for all concerned with the future of our troubled world.

Contents:
- *The Arts of Mr. Hun Tun* by Mokusen Miyuiki
- *Wilderness and the Search for the Soul of Modern Man* by C. A. Meier
- *The Four Eagle Feathers* by Joseph L. Henderson
- *Ndumu to Inverness – the Story of a Personal Journey* by Ian Player
- *Nature, Psyche and a Healing Ceremony of the Xhosa* by M. Vera Bührmann
- *The Wilderness* by Rix Weaver
- *The Ranch Papers* by Jane Hollister Wheelwright
- *Appointment with a Rhinoceros* by Laurens van der Post
- *Nature Aphoristic (with an excerpt from Goethe)* by Sam Francis

144 pages, ISBN 3-85630-503-3 (paper), ISBN 3-85630-502-5 (hardcover)

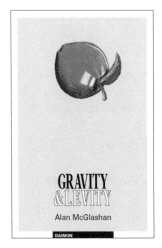

Alan McGlashan
Gravity and Levity
The Philosophy of Paradox

As the title suggests, this book addresses its subjects with wit and with weight, as the author brings the latest insights of contemporary physics into the perspective of an everyday life that is shown to be full of paradox. We can only come to terms with life if we accept that there are no final answers, and that unconscious processes are just as relevant as conscious ones. Reality cannot be anything but paradoxical, and our attitude to this fact has much to do with our state of being.

One of the most important books that has come my way for many years ... He is that rare phenomenon among men, one able to detect the movement of the spirit that could rid us of a crippling sense of meaninglessness and loss of purpose. – Laurens van der Post

162 pages, ISBN 3-85630-548-3

ENGLISH PUBLICATIONS BY **DAIMON**

ENGLISH PUBLICATIONS BY **DAIMON**

Laurens van der Post - *The Rock Rabbit and the Rainbow*

Jane Reid - *Jung, My Mother and I: The Analytic Diaries of Catharine Rush Cabot*

R.M. Rilke - *Duino Elegies*

Miguel Serrano - *C.G. Jung and Hermann Hesse*

Helene Shulman - *Living at the Edge of Chaos*

Dennis Slattery / Lionel Corbet (Eds.) - *Depth Psychology: Meditations on the Field*

Susan Tiberghien - *Looking for Gold*

Ann Ulanov - *The Wizards' Gate, Picturing Consciousness*
- *The Female Ancestors of Christ*
- *The Wisdom of the Psyche*

Ann & Barry Ulanov - *Cinderella and her Sisters: The Envied and the Envying*
- *Healing Imagination: Psyche and Soul*

Erlo van Waveren - *Pilgrimage to the Rebirth*

Harry Wilmer - *How Dreams Help*
- *Quest for Silence*

Luigi Zoja - *Drugs, Addiction and Initiation*

Jungian Congress Papers - *Jerusalem 1983: Symbolic and Clinical Approaches*
- *Berlin 1986: The Archetype of Shadow in a Split World*
- *Paris 1989: Dynamics in Relationship*
- *Chicago 1992: The Transcendent Function*
- *Zürich 1995: Open Questions*
- *Florence 1998: Destruction and Creation*

Available from your bookstore or from our distributors:

In the United States:

Continuum
22883 Quicksilver Drive
Dulles, VA 20166
Phone: 800-561 7704
Fax: 703-661 1501

Chiron Publications
400 Linden Avenue
Wilmette, IL 60091
Phone: 800-397 8109
Fax: 847-256 2202

In Great Britain:

Airlift Book Company
8 The Arena
Enfield, Middlesex EN3 7NJ
Phone: (0181) 804 0400
Fax: (0181) 804 0044

Worldwide:
Daimon Verlag   Hauptstrasse 85   CH-8840 Einsiedeln   Switzerland
Phone: (41)(55) 412 2266   Fax: (41)(55) 412 2231
email: info@daimon.ch

Visit our website: www.daimon.ch

or write for our complete catalog!